SCHOLASTIC

NO FUSS

ENGLISH
PHOTOCOPIABLES
AGES 7-11

LEVELS

■ **Levelled and linked to the curriculum**

D1580730

3-5

■ **Stand-alone photocopiable activities**

■ **Ideal for mixed-age classes**

Compiled by Alison Milford

CONTRIBUTORS

Text © **Diana Bentley and Dee Reid**: 101, 102, 103, 106, 107, 113, 114, 117, 119, 120, 127

Text © **Philip Bowditch**: 49, 55, 61, 75, 77, 78, 79, 80, 81, 84, 90, 92, 93, 94, 95, 96, 97, 98, 99, 112, 115, 125

Text © **Kate Caton**: 76, 86, 104, 105, 109, 116, 118, 122, 124

Text © **William Edmonds**: 19, 22, 26, 32, 54, 56, 62, 64, 73, 88, 89, 111

Text © **Norma Gaunt and Jane Whitwell**: 27, 47, 48, 65, 87, 121

Text © **Wendy Helsby**: 15, 20, 21, 24, 28, 29, 30, 31, 35, 36, 60, 71, 83, 85, 91, 108

Text © **Rita Ray**: 18, 23, 25, 39, 50, 51, 52, 53, 57, 58, 63, 66, 68, 69, 70, 72, 74, 100, 110, 123, 126

Text © **Angela Redfern**: 16, 17, 33, 34, 37, 38, 40, 41, 42, 43, 44, 45, 46, 59, 67, 82

CONSULTANT EDITOR

Alison Milford

ASSISTANT EDITOR

Wendy Tse

DESIGNERS

Lapiz Digital

COVER DESIGN

Anna Oliwa

ILLUSTRATORS

Illustration © **Garry Davies**: 18, 23, 25, 39, 50, 51, 52, 53, 57, 58, 63, 66, 68, 69, 70, 72, 74, 100, 110, 123, 126

Illustration © **Roger Fereday**: 49, 55, 61, 75, 77, 78, 79, 80, 81, 84, 90, 92, 93, 94, 95, 96, 97, 98, 99, 112, 115, 125

Illustration © **Robin Lawrie**: 47, 48, 65, 87, 106, 113, 114, 119, 120, 121, 127

Illustration © **Oxford Illustrators**: 15, 20, 21, 24, 28, 29, 30, 31, 35, 36, 43, 44, 45, 46, 60, 71, 83, 85, 91, 108

Illustration © **Sharon Pallent**: 27, 101, 102, 103, 107, 117

Illustration © **Liz Thomas**: 16, 17, 19, 22, 26, 32, 33, 34, 37, 38, 40, 41, 42, 54, 56, 59, 62, 64, 67, 73, 82, 88, 89, 111

Text and illustration copyright in individual pages as per acknowledgements.
Compilation © 2006 Scholastic Ltd

Every effort has been made to trace all the copyright owners of material but there were a few cases where authors and illustrators were untraceable. Scholastic will be happy to correct any omissions in future printings.

Published by Scholastic Ltd
Villiers House
Clarendon Avenue
Leamington Spa
Warwickshire
CV32 5PR

www.scholastic.co.uk

Designed using Adobe InDesign

Printed by Bell & Bain Ltd, Glasgow

1 2 3 4 5 6 7 8 9   6 7 8 9 0 1 2 3 4 5

British Library Cataloguing-in-Publication Data

A catalogue record for this book is available from the British Library.

ISBN 0-439-96549-7

ISBN 978-0439-96549-1

Extracts from the National Literacy Strategy reproduced under the terms of HMSO Guidance
Note 8. © Crown copyright.

Photocopiable pages and original teachers' notes first published in *Dictionary skills, Reading for comprehension, Reading non-fiction* and *Writing non-fiction* (all first published 1994) from the Essentials for English series, and *Grammar* (1997), *Handwriting activities* (1993), *Language puzzles* (1993), *Spelling and language skills* (1993), *Story writing* (1997), *Vocabulary skills* (1995) and *Writing* (1992) from the Teacher Timesavers series.

SCHOLASTIC
www.scholastic.co.uk

CONTENTS

CONTENTS

INTRODUCTION

This book contains over 100 of some of the best literacy photocopiable sheets compiled from past editions of Scholastic's popular series Essentials for English and Teacher Timesavers. The photocopiable sheets cover a wide range of literacy skills for seven- to eleven-year-olds and can be used by individuals, small groups or as class activities.

Aims of the book

• To offer fun and stimulating activities that encourage children to learn a range of literacy skills.

• To provide accessible activities that cover the literacy requirements for children aged seven to eleven.

• To provide activities that can be used for children of different abilities.

• To stimulate children into learning and discovering more about a skill or concept.

• To provide simple and interesting activities that can be used as an introduction to a lesson or skill or as a way of consolidating skills and knowledge.

• To be used as a resource that can be incorporated quickly and effectively into a busy timetable.

• To offer activities that could be used as forms of assessment.

• To act as a resource that offers good-quality activities to fill in an unplanned time slot.

Using the book

The activities: The photocopiable activities in this book are arranged in the order of the three levels of the National Literacy Strategy – Word level work, Sentence level work and Text level work. The chapters cover: Phonics, spelling and vocabulary; Grammar and punctuation; Comprehension and composition – fiction and poetry; Comprehension and composition – non-fiction. The activities progress throughout the chapters to match the children's development.

Curriculum grids: At the beginning of the book there are sets of curriculum grids which provide quick and easy-to-read information about each of the photocopiable activities. Each curriculum grid has seven sections:

Page number: This column indicates the page number of an activity for quick reference.

Activity: This column highlights the title of the activity.

Objective: This column highlights the specific objectives of an activity and what the children should be aiming to achieve

Teachers' notes: This column gives teachers advice about how to use an activity with the children. This could include how children should be using the activity, ways to introduce the activity, ways to extend the activity once it has been completed or ideas for differentiation.

Curriculum links: The last three columns give direct links to the relevant Government documents for the NLS and Scottish curriculum and attainment target levels for each activity. These links can help teachers include the activities in their planning, assessment and with the development of ideas for future relevant activities.

It has been fun compiling some of Scholastic's best photocopiable English activities and we hope you and the children have just as much fun and enjoyment using them.

Page	Activity	Objective	Teachers' notes	National Literacy Strategy links	Scottish Curriculum links	KS2 Levels
page 15	Muddled names	To use visual skills to decide if words look right.	Answers: Pied Piper; Charming; Aladdin; Cinderella; Snow White; Red Riding Hood; Robin Hood; Tom Thumb; King Arthur.	Y3 T1 Word 5; T2 Word 6; T3 Word 6; T3 Text 12 Y4 T1 Word 3; T2 Word 3; T3 Word 3	Writing: Spelling – Level C/D	AT2 Reading – Level 3/4 AT3 Writing – Level 3/4
page 16	Opposites	To investigate words starting with the prefixes 'in-', 'im-', 'ir-', and 'il-'.	Ensure that the children understand that prefixes are put at the front of words. Collect the list of the children's 'in-' words and display them so that more can be added. Answers: (List 1) inaccurate; incapable; inconsiderate; incredible; independent; indirect; illegal; illogical; impolite; impossible; improbable; irregular. (List 2) immobile; inattentive; incorrect; inadequate; infinite; imperfect; inexpensive; irresponsible; inconvenient; incomplete.	Y3 T1 Word 10; T2 Word 24 Y5 T2 Word 10; T3 Word 7	Writing: Spelling and Knowledge about language – Level D/E	AT2 Reading – Level 3/4/5 AT3 Writing – Level 3/4/5
page 17	Number puzzles	To investigate words starting with the prefixes 'uni-', 'bi-', 'tri-' and 'dec-'.	Highlight that these prefixes have their origins from the ancient Roman language Latin. Answers: triangle; tricycle; tripod; tricolour; trident; trio; trillion; triplets.	Y5 T3 Word 8 Y6 T1 Word 5	Writing: Spelling and Knowledge about language – Level D/E Reading: Reading for information – Level D/E	AT2 Reading – Level 4/5 AT3 Writing – Level 4/5
page 18	Family trees	To investigate words ending with the suffixes, '-ward', '-less', '-ness', '-ish', '-ly', '-ing', '-ed' and '-ful'.	Highlight how words with new meanings may be formed when suffixes are added to root words.	Y3 T2 Word 13, 14, 16 Y4 T1 Word 9; T2 Word 13	Writing: Spelling and Knowledge about language – Level C/D/E	AT2 Reading – Level 3/4/5 AT3 Writing – Level 3/4/5
page 19	Become a tryer, thinker, writer...	To understand that the suffix '-er' changes certain verbs into nouns.	Before or after the activity, go through some examples of verbs turned into nouns using '-er'.	Y3 T2 Word 8	Writing: Spelling and Knowledge about language – Level C/D/E	AT2 Reading – Level 3/4/5 AT3 Writing – Level 3/4/5
page 20	Shhh...	To investigate words that contain silent letters.	Support children by doing a few examples first. Wordsearch answers: writhe; awry; feign; write; corps; wrapped; psalms; design; ought; know.	Y3 T2 Word 10	Writing: Spelling and Knowledge about language – Level C/D/E	AT2 Reading – Level 3/4 AT3 Writing – Level 3/4
page 21	Speed trap	To find words that contain at least three letters from a larger word.	This activity would work best in pairs or in teams of three. Give the children a few sheets of paper to help them to work out the words.	Y3 T3 Word 8	Writing: Spelling and Knowledge about language – Level C/D/E Reading: Knowledge about language – Level C	AT2 Reading – Level 3/4/5 AT3 Writing – Level 3/4/5
page 22	Instead of 'said'	To use different words instead of 'said' in a given text.	The text is a piece of dialogue. Let children read it out first before they work on it. Have a thesaurus available.	Y3 T1 Word 19 Y3 T1 Sentence 3 Y4 T2 Sentence 9	Writing: Knowledge about language – Level C/D Reading: Knowledge about language – Level C/D	AT2 Reading – Level 3/4 AT3 Writing – Level 3/4
page 23	Nice words	To use a thesaurus to find alternative words to 'nice'.	After the activity ask the children to think of other common words that we use a lot and to think of or look for alternatives in a thesaurus.	Y3 T1 Word 16, 17, 18 Y4 T2 Text 9 Y5 T1 Text 24	Writing: Knowledge about language – Level C/D/E Reading: Knowledge about language – Level C/D/E	AT2 Reading – Level 3/4 AT3 Writing – Level 3/4
page 24	Synonyms	To investigate synonyms.	Show children a thesaurus and discuss how it helps them find words with similar meanings. Compare the synonyms that the children find for the list of words. Answers: dull/dowdy; aid/help; shout/bawl; hug/cuddle; mop/wipe; ooze/weep.	Y3 T1 Word 16, 17, 18 Y3 T3 Word 13 Y5 T1 Word 7	Writing: Knowledge about language – Level C/D/E Reading: Knowledge about language – Level C/D/E	AT2 Reading – Level 3/4/5 AT3 Writing – Level 3/4/5
page 25	Alphabetical order	To put words in alphabetical order up to the fourth letter.	The page could be stuck into the back of a child's book and used to check knowledge of alphabetical order.	Y3 T1 Word 15; T2 Word 22, 23 Y4 T1 Word 12	Writing: Knowledge about language – Level C/D/E Reading: Knowledge about language – Level C/D/E	AT2 Reading – Level 3/4/5 AT3 Writing – Level 3/4/5
page 26	A part-of-speech survey	To use the dictionary to find the frequencies of different words.	This activity allows the children to study the dictionary and understand its abbreviations. The children need to record the frequencies of words using an appropriate method.	Y3 T1 Word 15; T2 Word 19, 20, 21, 22, 23; T3 Word 15 Y5 T3 Word 11, 12	Writing: Knowledge about language – Level C/D/E Reading: Knowledge about language – Level C/D/E	AT2 Reading – Level 3/4/5 AT3 Writing – Level 3/4/5
page 27	Close clues	To use a dictionary to encourage scanning.	This activity will help children to focus on a page within a dictionary, as the words are close to each other.	Y3 T1 Word 15; T2 Word 19, 20, 21, 22, 23; T3 Word 15	Writing: Knowledge about language – Level C/D/E Reading: Knowledge about language – Level C/D/E	AT2 Reading – Level 3/4/5 AT3 Writing – Level 3/4/5

SCHOLASTIC www.scholastic.co.uk

Page	Activity	Objective	Teachers' notes	National Literacy Strategy links	Scottish Curriculum links	KS2 Levels
page 28	Cracker word puzzles	To investigate words that are homophones.	If possible, collect more jokes that involve homophones to provide more examples for the children. Answers: 1) flee; 2) skull; 3) brake; 4) coop; 5) four; 6) bean; 7) pail; 8) bare; 9) two.	**Y3** T3 Text 6 **Y4** T1 Word 6 **Y5** T2 Word 6	Writing: Knowledge about language – Level C/D/E Reading: Knowledge about language – Level C/D/E	AT2 Reading – Level 3/4/5 AT3 Writing – Level 3/4/5
page 29	Stepladders	To investigate compound words.	This is quite a fun but complicated activity and will need to be explained before the children start.	**Y3** T2 Word 12 **Y4** T3 Word 11	Writing: Knowledge about language – Level C/D/E Reading: Knowledge about language – Level C/D/E	AT2 Reading – Level 3/4/5 AT3 Writing – Level 3/4/5
page 30	Word wall	To investigate polysyllabic words.	Highlight how words are combined and how longer words can be broken into syllables to help spelling and reading. Answers: **bitten/tenant; guineapig/pigsty; shameless/lesson; pumpkin/kinship; wayout/outlet; tabor/orbit; bidden/denounce; pardon/donate; passport/porthole; bargain/gainfully.**	**Y5** T3 Word 4 **Y6** T3 Word 7	Writing: Knowledge about language – Level C/D/E Reading: Knowledge about language – Level C/D/E	AT2 Reading – Level 4/5 AT3 Writing – Level 4/5
page 31	Seeing double	To investigate words that have the double letters 'dd', 'gg', 'mm', 'nn' and 'pp'.	Answers: hammer; beginning; biggest; supper; middle; swimming; slipper.	**Y4** T1 Word 5	Writing: Spelling and Knowledge about language – Level C/D	AT2 Reading – Level 3/4 AT3 Writing – Level 3/4
page 32	Is it 'it's' or 'its'?	To learn to use 'it's' and 'its' correctly.	Before starting the activity, remind children that 'it's' stands for 'it is' while 'its' is to do with belonging: something that belongs to 'it'.	**Y4** T3 Word 10	Writing: Spelling and Knowledge about language – Level C/D/E	AT2 Reading – Level 3/4/5 AT3 Writing – Level 3/4/5
page 33	WPC Clough in action	To investigate the word root 'ough'.	Discuss different 'ough' words. Highlight that they may have the same word root, but they may be pronounced differently. Answers: 1) examples include Peterborough and Slough; 2) bough; 3) tougher; 4) coughing; 5) ought; 6) ploughed, rough; 7) enough.	**Y4** T3 Word 6 **Y5** T1 Text 21;T2 Word 5	Writing: Spelling and Knowledge about language – Level D/E	AT2 Reading – Level 4/5 AT3 Writing – Level 4/5
page 34	Doubling up	To find out how the end letters of some words double up when the suffixes 'ing' or 'ed' are added on.	Check the children understand the meanings of the words used in the activity. Discuss the different tenses used.	**Y3** T1 Word 8 **Y5** T2 Word 4;T3 Word 6	Writing: Spelling and Knowledge about language – Level C/D/E	AT2 Reading – Level 3/4/5 AT3 Writing – Level 3/4/5
page 35	Night and day	To investigate words that have opposite meanings.	Across answers: 1) last; 4) top; 5) slows; 7) night. Down answers: 2) strong; 3) to; 5) sun; 6) sit.	**Y3** T2 Word 24 **Y4** T2 Word 9 **Y5** T2 Word 10	Writing: Spelling and Knowledge about language – Level C/D/E	AT2 Reading – Level 3/4/5 AT3 Writing – Level 3/4/5
page 36	Homonyms	To investigate homonyms and use them to complete sentences.	Give children paper, pencils and rulers to make their homonym crosswords. Collect and write down the 'hand' sayings. Answers: minute; record; interest.	**Y3** T3 Word 14 **Y5** T2 Word 6 **Y6** T3 Word 7	Writing: Spelling and Knowledge about language – Level C/D/E	AT2 Reading – Level 4/5 AT3 Writing – Level 3/4/5
page 37	Figures of speech	To find out about figures of speech and what they mean.	Put the children into pairs to discuss the sayings. Highlight modern figures of speech or sayings that are part of their locality.	**Y5** T2 Word 12	Writing: Spelling and Knowledge about language – Level D/E Reading: Knowledge about language D/E	AT2 Reading – Level 4/5 AT3 Writing – Level 4/5
page 38	Daily bread	To be aware of how words from around the world are used in our vocabulary.	Go through the list of bread with children before they start the activity to discuss the different examples. Bring in examples to see which types of bread the children recognise and discuss where the breads or words originate.	**Y5** T2 Word 9;T3 Word 8, 9	Writing: Spelling and Knowledge about language – Level D/E Reading: Knowledge about language D/E	AT2 Reading – Level 4/5 AT3 Writing – Level 4/5
page 39	Word origins	To understand that words have different origins and to understand the word 'etymology'.	Encourage children to use an etymological dictionary to find word origins and point out that they may come up with different information.	**Y3** T3 Word 15 **Y6** T1 Word 10;T2 Word 5	Writing: Spelling and Knowledge about language – Level D/E Reading: Knowledge about language D/E	AT2 Reading – Level 4/5 AT3 Writing – Level 4/5

Page	Activity	Objective	Teachers' notes	National Literacy Strategy links	Scottish Curriculum links	KS2 Levels
page 40	A changing language	To learn how words and expressions have changed over time or fallen out of use.	Read the extract out loud. Do the children find it easier to recognise or translate the words by listening to them or by looking at and reading them? As an extension, let the children translate the Chaucer into modern-day English.	Y4 T2 Word 11; Y6 T1 Word 7	Writing: Spelling and Knowledge about language – Level D/E; Reading: Knowledge of language – Level D/E	AT2 Reading – Level 4/5; AT3 Writing – Level 4/5
page 41	Proverbs	To look at proverbs and their meanings from another culture.	Ask the children if they know of proverbs from other cultures and put a collection together.	Y6 T2 Word 6; T3 Sentence 2	Writing: Knowledge about language – Level D/E; Reading: Knowledge of language – Level D/E	AT2 Reading – Level 4/5; AT3 Writing – Level 4/5
page 42	Similes	To understand what similes and clichés are.	Highlight to the children that the first list of similes must be written down as fast as they can. Compare the two lists at the end.	Y5 T2 Word 9; Y6 T3 Word 7	Writing Knowledge about language – Level D/E; Reading: Knowledge of language – Level D/E	AT2 Reading – Level 4/5; AT3 Writing – Level 4/5
page 43	Floorboards	To practise correct formation of diagonal and horizontal joins.	Go over the four-step routine with the children: 1) write over word; 2) look, cover and write from memory; 3) check then write it again; 4) write with eyes closed.	Y3 T1-3 Word – Handwriting; Y4 T1-3 Word – Handwriting	Writing: Handwriting – Level C/D/E	AT3 Writing – Level 3/4/5
page 44	Build a wall	To practise correct formation of diagonal and horizontal joins.	Ask children to make another wall with more four-letter words. Highlight the need to use the four-step routine (see above).	Y3 T1-3 Word – Handwriting; Y4 T1-3 Word – Handwriting	Writing: Handwriting – Level C/D/E	AT3 Writing – Level 3/4/5
page 45	Hissing sounds	To practise the joining technique for the letter 's'.	Emphasis the need to practise the 'ss' on the snake before copying out the words.	Y3 T1-3 Word – Handwriting; Y4 T1-3 Word – Handwriting	Writing: Handwriting – Level C/D/E	AT3 Writing – Level 3/4/5
page 46	Bashful is...	To practise the correct formation of the letters 'full'.	This is a good activity to practise collecting and using words with the same suffix. Highlight the need for neat work.	Y3 T3 Word 13; Y1-3 Word – Handwriting; Y4 T1-3 Word – Handwriting	Writing: Handwriting – Level C/D/E	AT3 Writing – Level 3/4/5
page 47	A pony and trap ride	To predict and add verbs into a text.	This passage is from The Secret Garden by Frances Hodgson Burnett. Encourage children to make lists of suitable verbs before they choose the final ones for the text. The missing words from the original text are: arrived, was, discover, curled, kept, cast, caught, drove, saw, passed, noticed, began, were, hear.	Y3 T1 Sentence 1, 3, 4, 5; T2 Sentence 1; T3 Sentence 1; Y4 T1 Sentence 3	Writing: Imaginative writing – Level C/D; Reading: Awareness of genre – Level C/D	AT2 Reading – Level 3/4; AT3 Writing – Level 3/4
page 48	A wartime memory	To correctly sequence paragraphs of a written text.	Make sure the children read out the paragraphs first before they decide on the correct order. Sequenced order: 3, 1, 6, 4, 2, 5.	Y4 T2 Sentence 3; T3 Text 3; Y5 T1 Text 4; Y6 T2 Text 2	Writing: Imaginative writing – Level C/D/E; Reading: Awareness of genre – Level C/D/E	AT2 Reading – Level 3/4/5; AT3 Writing – Level 3/4/5
page 49	Direct speech	To recognise the rules of and to set out direct speech.	Read children an extract with direct speech from a story. Ask children to identify where speech marks should start and finish.	Y3 T1 Sentence 2, 7, 8, Text 2, 10; T3 Sentence 4; Y5 T1 Text 3	Writing: Punctuation and structure and Knowledge about language – C/D/E; Reading: Knowledge about language – Level C/D/E	AT2 Reading – Level 3/4/5; AT3 Writing – Level 3/4/5
page 50	Direct and indirect	To understand the difference between direct and reported speech.	This activity gives children models to support the task of putting a piece of dialogue into indirect speech.	Y3 T1 Sentence 2, 7, 8; T3 Sentence 4; Y5 T1 Sentence 5, 7	Writing: Punctuation and structure and Knowledge about language – Level D/E; Reading: Knowledge about language – Level D/E	AT2 Reading – Level 4/5; AT3 Writing – Level 4/5
page 51	Shock horror game!	To use exclamation marks appropriately.	Check that children understand why exclamation marks are used and how they could be used in the game.	Y3 T1 Sentence 2; T2 Text 16; Y4 T3 Sentence 3; Y5 T1 Sentence 6, Text 25	Writing: Punctuation and structure and Knowledge about language – C/D/E; Reading: Knowledge about language – Level C/D/E	AT2 Reading – Level 3/4; AT3 Writing – Level 3/4
page 52	Time to pause	To learn how commas can be used to show where to pause in a text.	Before the activity you may want to read through a story extract without commas and then with commas so that children can hear the difference.	Y3 T1 Sentence 2; T2 Sentence 6, 7; Y4 T1 Sentence 5; T2 Sentence 4; Y5 T1 Sentence 6	Writing: Punctuation and structure and Knowledge about language – Level D/E; Reading: Knowledge about language – Level D/E	AT2 Reading – Level 3/4/5; AT3 Writing – Level 3/4/5
page 53	Agreeable verbs	To look at the concept of subject-verb agreement.	Children should read out the sentences before they write down the correct sentences, so that they can recognise the correct verbs.	Y3 T1 Sentence 3; T2 Sentence 4; Y4 T3 Sentence 3; Y5 T1 Sentence 2, 8	Writing: Punctuation and structure and Knowledge about language – Level D/E; Reading: Knowledge about language – Level D/E	AT2 Reading – Level 4/5; AT3 Writing – Level 4/5

SCHOLASTIC
www.scholastic.co.uk

Page	Activity	Objective	Teachers' notes	National Literacy Strategy links	Scottish Curriculum links	KS2 Levels
page 54	Kate's big ed-venture	To recognise how the regular past tense works by adding '-ed'.	The story in this activity is filled with misspellings and it challenges children to find the correct irregular past tense verb.	Y4 T1 Word 7, 8, Sentence 2, 3; Y5 T1 Sentence 8	Writing: Spelling and Knowledge about language – Level C/D; Reading: Knowledge about language – Level C/D	AT2 Reading – Level 3/4; AT3 Writing – Level 3/4
page 55	Story tenses	To write story texts using past or present tenses.	Review the difference between past and present tense with children before they start the activity.	Y4 T1 Word 7, Sentence 2; T3 Sentence 3; Y5 T1 Sentence 8; T3 Word 6	Writing: Knowledge about language – Level D/E; Reading: Knowledge about language – Level D/E	AT2 Reading – Level 3/4/5; AT3 Writing – Level 3/4/5
page 56	Funny faces	To use adjectives to describe faces.	This activity has a selection of adjectives from which children can choose in order to label a row of funny faces.	Y3 T2 Sentence 2, 3	Writing: Knowledge about language – Level C/D; Reading: Knowledge about language – Level C/D	AT2 Reading – Level 3/4; AT3 Writing – Level 3/4
page 57	Messy, messier, messiest	To investigate ways of using adjectives by adding on the suffixes '-ier', '-iest', '-er' and '-est'.	Ask children to read out the words on the table so that they can hear the right use of suffixes to put on the end.	Y3 T2 Sentence 2, 3; Y4 T2 Sentence 1; Y5 T3 Word 6	Writing: Spelling and Knowledge about language – Level C/D/E; Reading: Knowledge about language – Level C/D/E	AT2 Reading – Level 4/5; AT3 Writing – Level 4/5
page 58	You're the most	To use superlative adjectives for expressive language in poems.	Explain that the superlative of an adjective describes the very best or highest quality of something, for example, juiciest or sweetest.	Y3 T2 Sentence 2, 3; Y4 T2 Sentence 1, Text 11, 13	Writing: Spelling and Knowledge about language – Level D/E; Reading: Knowledge about language – Level D/E	AT2 Reading – Level 4/5; AT3 Writing – Level 4/5
page 59	Two by two	To explore the plural endings of different words.	This activity could be used as an assessment or consolidation of the children's knowledge of the different forms of plurals. Answers: asses; buffaloes; foxes; monkeys; mosquitoes; wives; ponies; wolves; oxen; mice; geese; cherries; matches; boxes; knives; spoons; loaves; potatoes; tomatoes; shoes; brushes; dominoes; shelves.	Y3 T2 Sentence 4, 5	Writing: Spelling and Knowledge about language – Level C/D; Reading: Knowledge about language – Level C/D	AT2 Reading – Level 3/4; AT3 Writing – Level 3/4
page 60	Collectomania	To understand the term 'collective noun' and collect examples.	Ask the children if they know any collective nouns already and challenge them to find new and unusual ones. Across answers: 3) shoal; 4) quiver; 6) litter; 7) gaggle. Down answers: 1) school; 2) bouquet; 5) flight.	Y3 T2 Sentence 4, 5	Writing: Spelling and Knowledge about language – Level C/D; Reading: Knowledge about language – Level D/E	AT2 Reading – Level 3/4; AT3 Writing – Level 3/4
page 61	Conjunctions	To understand the term 'conjunction' and use them in a given text.	Before the activity, read two sentences and ask children to suggest a conjunction to join them.	Y3 T3 Sentence 5, 6; Y4 T2 Sentence 3, 4; Y5 T3 Sentence 7; Y6 T1 Sentence 4, 5	Writing: Punctuation and structure and Knowledge about language – Level D/E; Reading: Knowledge about language – Level D/E	AT2 Reading – Level 3/4/5; AT3 Writing – Level 3/4/5
page 62	Finding personal pronouns	To recognise and use personal pronouns.	This activity invites children to use eleven basic personal pronouns (I, me, he, she, him, her, we, us, you, they, them).	Y3 T3 Sentence 2, 3; Y5 T2 Word 7, Sentence 3, 10	Writing: Punctuation and structure and Knowledge about language – Level D/E; Reading: Knowledge about language – Level D/E	AT2 Reading – Level 3/4/5; AT3 Writing – Level 3/4/5
page 63	Underlining adverbs	To recognise adverbs in a text and use them for finishing off a story.	Remind children that adverbs tell you how something is done. Highlight how adverbs end with the suffix '-ly'.	Y4 T1 Sentence 4	Writing: Spelling and Knowledge about language – Level D/E; Reading: Knowledge about language – Level D/E	AT2 Reading – Level 4/5; AT3 Writing – Level 4/5
page 64	Tremendously revealing comments	To use adverbs and adjectives to express feelings about different issues.	After the activity, ask the children to read out their sentences and list the adverbs and adjectives.	Y4 T1 Sentence 4; T2 Sentence 1	Writing: Spelling and Knowledge about language – Level D/E; Reading: Knowledge about language – Level D/E	AT2 Reading – Level 4/5; AT3 Writing – Level 4/5
page 65	Holiday at sea	To find suitable adverbs for a given text.	This passage is from Swallows and Amazons by Arthur Ransome. Encourage children to make lists of suitable adverbs before they choose the final ones for the text. The missing words from the original text are: tidily; gently; slowly; quickly; excitedly; steadily; loudly; eagerly; happily; uncontrollably; wearily.	Y4 T1 Sentence 4; Y5 T1 Word 10	Writing: Imaginative writing and Knowledge of language – Level D/E; Reading: Awareness of genre and Knowledge of language – Level D/E	AT2 Reading – Level 4/5; AT3 Writing – Level 4/5

Page	Activity	Objective	Teachers' notes	National Literacy Strategy links	Scottish Curriculum links	KS2 Levels
page 66	Spot the apostrophes	To understand rules for apostrophising singular and plural nouns.	Children may want to draw pictures to go with their examples of apostrophes.	Y4 T2 Sentence 2; Y5 T3 Sentence 5	Writing: Spelling and Knowledge about language – Level D/E; Reading: Knowledge about language – Level D/E	AT2 Reading – Level 4/5; AT3 Writing – Level 4/5
page 67	Apostrophes	To use apostrophes for contracting words.	Highlight how we use apostrophes in informal writing to cut down words. You may want to write some examples before the activity.	Y3 T2 Word 15; T3 Word 11; Y4 T2 Sentence 2	Writing: Spelling and Knowledge about language – Level D/E; Reading: Knowledge about language – Level D/E	AT2 Reading – Level 4/5; AT3 Writing – Level 4/5
page 68	What's the big idea?	To understand the difference between a main clause and a subordinate clause.	Before the activity, write a few simple sentences and highlight the main clauses and subordinate clauses.	Y5 T3 Sentence 6, 7; Y6 T2 Sentence 3	Writing: Punctuation and structure and Knowledge about language – Level D/E; Reading: Knowledge about language – Level D/E	AT2 Reading – Level 4/5; AT3 Writing – Level 4/5
page 69	Put them together	To see how main clauses and subordinate clause can be joined to make a sentence.	As an extension ask the children to write fun main and subordinate clauses and match them up.	Y5 T3 Sentence 6, 7; Y6 T2 Sentence 3	Writing: Punctuation and structure and Knowledge about language – Level D/E; Reading: Knowledge about language – Level D/E	AT2 Reading – Level 4/5; AT3 Writing – Level 4/5
page 70	Pick and mix	To look at the names and functions of parts of speech and construction of sentences.	This activity can be done in pairs or in small groups where the cards can be used to play a 'Happy Families' type game.	Y5 T2 Sentence 8	Writing: Punctuation and structure and Knowledge about language – Level D/E; Reading: Knowledge about language – Level D/E	AT2 Reading – Level 4/5; AT3 Writing – Level 4/5
page 71	Sentencestics	To use a set amount of words to make a sentence.	Explain how acrostics work before children start on the puzzle. Acrostics are a system of words across placed to make a word down. Answers: 1) today; 2) some; 3) at; 4) school; 5) taught; 6) lessons; 7) our; 8) us; 9) teachers.	Y5 T2 Sentence 8	Writing: Punctuation and structure and Knowledge about language – Level D/E; Reading: Knowledge about language – Level D/E	AT2 Reading – Level 4/5; AT3 Writing – Level 4/5
page 72	Banana split	To be aware of the differences between spoken and written language.	This task focuses on the difference between spoken and written language. Children are asked to take the facts from an oral account about a recipe and turn them into a set of instructions.	Y4 T1 Text 22, 25; Y5 T2 Sentence 1	Writing: Knowledge about language – Level D/E; Reading: Knowledge about language – Level C/D/E	AT2 Reading – Level 4/5; AT3 Writing – Level 4/5
page 73	Which way is it?	To use prepositions for directions.	Ask children to think of suitable directional prepositions to guide Anwar to school as shown on a simple map.	Y5 T1 Text 25; T3 Sentence 3; Y6 T1 Sentence 4	Writing: Functional writing – Level D/E; Reading: Reading for information – Level D/E	AT2 Reading – Level 4/5; AT3 Writing – Level 4/5
page 74	Put it where!	To use prepositions to explain where something is.	For longer use of the activity, photocopy the picture and let children cut out the objects to place on the picture.	Y5 T3 Sentence 3; Y6 T1 Sentence 4	Writing: Functional writing – Level D/E; Reading: Reading for information – Level D/E	AT2 Reading – Level 4/5; AT3 Writing – Level 4/5
page 75	Aircraft story	To be aware of how dialogue is presented in stories.	Draw children's attention to the aircraft language in the box on the sheet. Outline briefly how a plane is controlled and explain that the airport control tower will give the pilot instructions about how to land the aircraft. Encourage children to empathise with the passenger's feeling.	Y3 T1 Text 2, 4, 10; T3 Text 5; Y4 T2 Text 9; Y5 T1 Text 3, 11	Writing: Imaginative writing – Level C/D; Reading: Awareness of genre and Knowledge about language – Level C/D; Talking: Knowledge about language – Level C/D/E; Listening: Listening in order to respond to texts – Level C/D/E	AT1 Speaking and listening – Level 3/4/5; AT2 Reading – Level 3/4/5; AT3 Writing – Level 3/4/5
page 76	Let's talk!	To write simple playscripts of dialogue for a performance.	Explain to children how to write dialogue. A discussion about use of speech marks and drama format would be useful.	Y3 T1 Text 2, 4; T3 Text 5; Y4 T1 Text 5, 13; Y5 T1 Text 3, 11	Writing: Imaginative writing – Level C/D; Reading: Awareness of genre and Knowledge about language – Level C/D; Talking: Knowledge about language – Level C/D; Listening: Listening in order to respond to texts – Level C/D/E	AT1 Speaking and listening – Level 3/4/5; AT2 Reading – Level 3/4/5; AT3 Writing – Level 3/4/5
page 77	Paragraphs	To understand why and where paragraphs are used.	Before starting the activity, explain when and why writers use paragraphs and how these are indicated (indent, extra line space).	Y3 T1 Text 16; T3 Text 13; Y4 T1 Text 15; T3 Text 3	Writing: Punctuation and structure – Level C/D; Reading: Knowledge about language – Level C/D	AT2 Reading – Level 3/4/5; AT3 Writing – Level 3/4/5
page 78	Which person?	To distinguish between first- and third-person accounts.	Ask children which style of writing they would use to write different types stories, such as scary stories or fairy tales, and why.	Y3 T3 Text 3, 12	Writing: Imaginative writing – Level D/E; Reading: Awareness of genre and Knowledge about language – Level D/E	AT2 Reading – Level 3/4/5; AT3 Writing – Level 3/4/5

SCHOLASTIC
www.scholastic.co.uk

Page	Activity	Objective	Teachers' notes	National Literacy Strategy links	Scottish Curriculum links	KS2 Levels
page 79	Ordering chapter headings	To understand how chapters are used to collect, order and build up ideas.	Cut out the chapter headings on the sheet beforehand so that children can experiment with different orders before they write down their answers.	Y3 T3 Text 1 Y4 T3 Text 3	Writing: Punctuation and structure and Knowledge about language – Level C/D/E Reading: Awareness of genre and Knowledge about language – Level C/D/E	AT2 Reading – Level 3/4/5 AT3 Writing – Level 3/4/5
page 80	Writing chapter headings	To understand how chapters are used to collect, order and build up ideas.	Go through the first two parts of the story outline and ask children for suggestions for chapter headings.	Y3 T3 Text 1 Y4 T3 Text 3 Y6 T1 Text 8	Writing: Punctuation and structure and Knowledge about language – Level C/D/E Reading: Awareness of genre and Knowledge about language – Level C/D/E	AT2 Reading – Level 3/4/5 AT3 Writing – Level 3/4/5
page 81	The message	To use stimulus to write a science fiction story.	Check that the children understand how to use the decoder by writing words for them to translate.	Y3 T3 Text 11 Y4 T2 Text 1 Y5 T1 Text 1 Y6 T2 Text 10	Writing: Imaginative writing – Level C/D/E Reading: Knowledge about language – Level C/D/E	AT2 Reading – Level 3/4/5 AT3 Writing – Level 3/4/5
page 82	Fun with puns	To investigate and use puns.	Read out a few puns before the activity so the children understand the idea behind them.	Y3 T3 Text 6 Y5 T1 Text 8	Writing: Knowledge about language – Level C/D/E Reading: Knowledge about language – Level C/D/E	AT2 Reading – Level 3/4/5 AT3 Writing – Level 3/4/5
page 83	Palindromes: ←this way, that way→ ←either way→	To understand what a palindrome is.	Ensure that the children understand what a palindrome is before they start this activity. Does anyone in the class have a palindromic name? Answers: 1) noon; 2) ewe; 3) radar; 4) pop; 5) nun; 6) kayak; 7) eve; 8) pip. My name is Anna. Eve is the first woman in the Bible.	Y3 T3 Text 6 Y5 T1 Text 8	Writing: Knowledge about language – Level C/D/E Reading: Knowledge about language – Level C/D/E	AT2 Reading – Level 3/4/5 AT3 Writing – Level 3/4/5
page 84	Scary alliteration	To understand alliteration and use it for description.	Explain what alliteration is and recite an example such as: 'Peter Piper picked a peck of pickled pepper.' Discuss the effects created by the use of alliteration in writing.	Y3 T3 Text 6 Y5 T1 Text 8	Writing: Knowledge about language – Level C/D/E Reading: Knowledge about language – Level C/D/E	AT2 Reading – Level 3/4/5 AT3 Writing – Level 3/4/5
page 85	A rhyming puzzle	To understand that rhyming words sound the same but do not have to be spelled in the same way.	Highlight that rhyming words do not have to be spelled in the same way. Show some examples to the children. Answers: noose/goose; high/die; hair/care; you/flew; pail/sale; house/mouse; seat/feet. The weather might change today.	Y3 T1 Text 7 Y4 T1 Text 14;T3 Text 4, 6,	Writing: Knowledge about language – Level C/D/E Reading: Knowledge about language – Level C/D/E	AT2 Reading – Level 3/4/5 AT3 Writing – Level 3/4/5
page 86	My farm-i-o!	To identify different patterns of verse and chorus in poetry.	Talk about the pattern of the chorus and verse and let the children identify the rhyming words.	Y4 T2 Text 7, 11;T3 Text 7	Writing: Knowledge about language – Level C/D/E Reading: Awareness of genre and Knowledge about language – Level C/D/E	AT2 Reading – Level 3/4/5 AT3 Writing – Level 3/4/5
page 87	The thrushes' nest	To put a poem in correct sequence by following the rhyming pattern.	Put children in pairs. You can give out starting lines for this poem as the rhyming sequence is complex and difficult to predict. Sequenced order: 1, 3, 6, 2, 7, 5, 4.	Y4 T3 Text 4, 6 Y6 T3 Text 4	Writing: Punctuation and structure – Level D/E Reading: Awareness of genre – Level D/E	AT2 Reading – Level 4/5 AT3 Writing – Level 4/5
page 88	Like a volcano	To use expressive language for poetry.	Have a thesaurus and dictionary on hand for children to look up words they may need for their poem.	Y3 T1 Text 13 Y4 T1 Text 14;T2 Text 4, 13	Writing: Imaginative writing – Level C/D/E Reading: Awareness of genre and Knowledge about language – Level C/D/E	AT2 Reading – Level 3/4/5 AT3 Writing – Level 3/4/5
page 89	Like a beautiful bird	To use expressive language to describe feelings.	The bird shape in this activity can be written upon, coloured, cut out, folded and hung up for display.	Y3 T1 Text 13 Y4 T1 Text 14;T2 Text 4, 13	Writing: Imaginative writing – Level C/D/E Reading: Awareness of genre and Knowledge about language – Level C/D/E	AT2 Reading – Level 3/4/5 AT3 Writing – Level 3/4/5
page 90	Weather myth	To identify that myths are sometimes used to explain natural events.	Explain the definition of a myth to the children. Give each group of children one type of weather on the sheet and ask them to devise a myth to explain it orally.	Y3 T2 Text 2, 6, 9, 10	Writing: Imaginative writing – Level C/D/E Reading: Awareness of genre and Knowledge about language – Level C/D/E	AT2 Reading – Level 3/4/5 AT3 Writing – Level 3/4/5
page 91	A mixed-up myth	To put a myth into the correct narrative sequence.	Children need to read the sentences first before they put them in sequence. Suggest they find the first and last sentence when they begin the activity. Answers: 1) c; 2) i; 3) h; 4) d; 5) b; 6) e; 7) g; 8) f; 9) a; 10) i; 11) k; 12) j.	Y4 T1 Text 4 Y5 T2 Text 1, 11 Y6 T2 Text 1	Writing: Punctuation and structure and Imaginative writing – Level D/E Reading: Awareness of genre and Knowledge about language – Level D/E	AT2 Reading – Level 4/5 AT3 Writing – Level 4/5

Page	Activity	Objective	Teachers' notes	National Literacy Strategy links	Scottish Curriculum links	KS2 Levels
page 92	Astronaut file	To write a character CV and list qualities.	Display pictures of astronauts. Discuss the kind of skills and personality an astronaut would need.	Y3 T2 Text 3, 9	Writing: Imaginative writing – Level C/D/E Reading: Awareness of genre and Knowledge about language – Level C/D/E	AT2 Reading – Level 3/4/5 AT3 Writing – Level 3/4/5
page 93	Characters in adventure stories	To look at typical characters in adventure stories.	Ask groups of children to list as many adventure story heroes/heroines and villains as they can.	Y3 T2 Text 3, 9; T3 Text 5 Y5 T1 Text 3; T2 Text 9	Writing: Imaginative writing – Level D/E Reading: Awareness of genre and Knowledge about language – Level D/E	AT2 Reading – Level 4/5 AT3 Writing – Level 4/5
page 94	Adventure story chart	To look at the different features of an adventure story.	Read extracts from an adventure story and ask children to identify relevant ingredients on the chart.	Y3 T1 Text 8 Y4 T2 Text 1, 2, 3, Y5 T1 Text 2; T2 Text 9 Y6 T2 Text 8	Writing: Imaginative writing – Level D/E Reading: Awareness of genre and Knowledge about language – Level D/E	AT2 Reading – Level 4/5 AT3 Writing – Level 4/5
page 95	Planet in danger story	To explore main issues and problems within a story.	Ask children to identify problems that people face on planet Earth and how these problems might be solved.	Y4 T3 Text 8, 11	Writing: Imaginative writing – Level D/E Reading: Awareness of genre and Knowledge about language – Level D/E	AT2 Reading – Level 4/5 AT3 Writing – Level 4/5
page 96	Pollution	To use a chart to plan a story about the problem of pollution.	Ask children to discuss causes and effects of different types of pollution, orally in groups, before they fill in the chart.	Y4 T3 Text 8, 11	Writing: Functional and Personal writing – Level D/E Reading: Reading for information – Level D/E	AT2 Reading – Level 4/5 AT3 Writing – Level 4/5
page 97	World War II diary	To write a first-person account in a diary form.	Discuss what life must have been like for the four characters on the sheet. Highlight how a diary is set out.	Y4 T1 Text 12 Y5 T1 Text 3; T3 Text 7 Y6 T1 Text 6	Writing: Imaginative writing – Level D/E Reading: Awareness of genre and Knowledge about language – Level D/E	AT2 Reading – Level 3/4/5 AT3 Writing – Level 3/4/5
page 98	Crime by numbers	To use different features to write a crime story.	With groups or the whole class, brainstorm possible objects, characters and crimes which could be incorporated in crime stories.	Y3 T2 Text 6, 7 Y4 T1 Text 9 Y6 T2 Text 7 10, 12	Writing: Imaginative writing – Level D/E Reading: Awareness of genre and Knowledge about language – Level D/E	AT2 Reading – Level 4/5 AT3 Writing – Level 4/5
page 99	Musical story	To set out ideas and research notes to write a story.	Highlight how research and notes help build up ideas for a story line. The sheet is a good model for this. Show the children a variety of musical instruments and let them hear what the instruments sound like.	Y3 T2 Text 6, 7 Y4 T2 Text 9, 10 Y6 T2 Text 7, 10, 12	Writing: Imaginative writing – Level D/E Reading: Awareness of genre and Knowledge about language – Level D/E	AT2 Reading – Level 4/5 AT3 Writing – Level 4/5
page 100	Finding your way around books	To understand the difference between fiction and non-fiction books.	Challenge children to draw some conclusions about the characteristics of fiction and non-fiction texts from their tick sheets.	Y3 T1 Text 17, 18, 19, 20; T3 Text 17, 18 Y4 T2 Text 15	Writing: Knowledge about language – Level C/D/E Reading: Awareness of genre and Knowledge about language – Level C/D/E	AT2 Reading – Level 3/4/5 AT3 Writing – Level 3/4/5
page 101	The platypus	To read information and underline main points of text.	Highlight how underlining text is a way of focusing attention upon specific aspects of the text. Labels: eggs; milk glands; webbed feet; soft bill; strong front limbs for paddling; strong hind legs for swimming; poison gland; furry body.	Y3 T1 Text 21 Y4 T2 Text 18, 23	Writing: Functional writing – Level C/D/E Reading: Reading for information – Level C/D/E	AT2 Reading – Level 3/4/5 AT3 Writing – Level 3/4/5
page 102	The human body	To organise and sort out the characteristics of an index page.	Give children different example of non-fiction books to study the layout of indices. They need to know that the topic words are in alphabetical order and are often in bold and that the sub-headings are listed below each topic word, also in alphabetical order.	Y3 T1 Text 19; T3 Text 24	Writing: Functional writing and Knowledge about language – Level C/D/E Reading: Reading for information and Knowledge about language – Level C/D/E	AT2 Reading – Level 3/4/5 AT3 Writing – Level 3/4/5
page 103	Elephants	To put given information on a chart.	Organising information into different forms of presentation is a good way to help concentration upon the subject matter. Possible headings for the elephant chart include: social grouping; senses; ears; backs; foreheads; tusks; nostrils.	Y3 T1 Text 21, 23 Y4 T2 Text 18, 23	Writing: Functional writing and Knowledge about language – Level C/D/E Reading: Reading for information and Knowledge about language – Level C/D/E	AT2 Reading – Level 3/4/5 AT3 Writing – Level 3/4/5
page 104	Taking exercise!	To make notes and produce a non-chronological report on exercise.	Highlight how the sheet helps children organise their ideas before writing a non-chronological report.	Y3 T1 Text 23	Writing: Functional writing and Knowledge about language – Level C/D/E Reading: Reading for information and Knowledge about language – Level C/D/E	AT2 Reading – Level 3/4/5 AT3 Writing – Level 3/4/5

SCHOLASTIC
www.scholastic.co.uk

Page	Activity	Objective	Teachers' notes	National Literacy Strategy links	Scottish Curriculum links	KS2 Levels
page 105	School pets	To make notes and produce a non-chronological report on pets.	If there is no school pet, the children could write about what pets they might like.	Y3 T1 Text 23	Writing: Functional writing – Level C/D/E Reading: Reading for information – Level C/D/E	AT2 Reading – Level 3/4/5 AT3 Writing – Level 3/4/5
page 106	Making a jelly	To write out a set of instructions for making a jelly.	Highlight the language and layout for writing a clear instructional text.	Y3 T2 Text 12, 14, 16 Y4 T1 Text 22, 25	Writing: Functional writing and Punctuation and structure – Level C/D/E Reading: Reading for information – Level C/D/E	AT2 Reading – Level 3/4/5 AT3 Writing – Level 3/4/5
page 107	Heraldry	To read a text of instructions to complete an illustration.	Children need to take their time over the shield. Let them make a rough sketch before completing the page. The children may need help understanding that all the shield details are from the point of view of the knight.	Y3 T2 Text 12, 14, 15	Reading: Reading for information – Level C/D/E	AT2 Reading – Level 3/4/5
page 108	The right order	To put instructions for a recipe into the right narrative sequence.	A fun follow-up activity would be to follow the instructions (in the right or wrong order!) to demonstrate the importance of putting instructions in the right narrative sequence, as well as including all the important steps. What happens if two steps were swapped or if one step was missed out? Answers: 1) i; 2) c; 3) e; 4) b; 5) h; 7) f; 8) n; 9) m; 10) l; 11) a; 12) g; 13) k; 14) d.	Y3 T2 Text 12, 14, 15, 16	Writing: Functional writing and Punctuation and structure – Level C/D/E Reading: Reading for information – Level C/D/E	AT2 Reading – Level 3/4/5 AT3 Writing – Level 3/4/5
page 109	What's the message?	To understand the importance of recording the main points of a message.	Taking a message in note form is an important skill. This exercise will show the children the importance of recording the main points of a message.	Y3 T2 Text 17 Y5 T1 Text 26	Writing: Functional writing and Knowledge about language – Level C/D/E Reading: Reading for information – Level C/D/E	AT2 Reading – Level 3/4/5 AT3 Writing – Level 3/4/5
page 110	Animal agony aunt	To present a point of view using a letter.	Explain how persuasive language highlights a point of view. Discuss the letters' points of view.	Y3 T3 Text 2, 16, 20, 23 Y4 T3 Text 18, 21, 23	Writing: Imaginative writing and Knowledge about language – Level C/D/E Reading: Reading for information – Level C/D/E	AT2 Reading – Level 3/4/5 AT3 Writing – Level 3/4/5
page 111	A request letter	To write a request letter using the correct form and layout.	This activity offers a range of phrases and vocabulary that might be useful for writing this type of letter.	Y3 T3 Text 16, 20, 23 Y5 T3 Text 17	Writing: Functional writing and Knowledge about language – Level C/D/E Reading: Reading for information and Knowledge about language – Level C/D/E	AT2 Reading – Level 4/5 AT3 Writing – Level 4/5
page 112	Changing places	To write a diary extract and recognise features of recounts.	Highlight the informal language and chronological features of writing diaries. Discuss who the children would most like to change places with and why.	Y3 T3 Text 22 Y5 T1 Text 24	Writing: Imaginative writing and Punctuation and structure – Level C/D/E Reading: Reading for information and Awareness of genre – Level C/D/E	AT2 Reading – Level 3/4/5 AT3 Writing – Level 3/4/5
page 113	The school outing	To write a recount of a school journey.	Go through the events on the sheet and highlight that they are in chronological order. Time-lines are designed to be a quick way of representing events in a chronological order and can be used to represent any length of time.	Y3 T3 Text 22 Y5 T1 Text 24	Writing: Functional writing and Punctuation and structure – Level C/D/E Reading: Reading for information – Level C/D/E	AT2 Reading – Level 4/5 AT3 Writing – Level 4/5
page 114	Fact or opinion? 'Children watch too much television'.	To understand and use the terms 'fact' and 'opinion'.	As an extension, let children look at newspaper articles to separate fact from opinion.	Y4 T1 Text 19, 24; T2 Text 18, 21	Writing: Functional writing and Knowledge about language – Level C/D/E Reading: Reading for information and Awareness of genre – Level C/D/E	AT2 Reading – Level 3/4/5 AT3 Writing – Level 3/4/5
page 115	Headline news	To write short headlines to get over a message.	Show children a range of newspaper headlines. Look at length and styles of the different headlines. Discuss whether the story behind the report is always clear from the headline.	Y4 T1 Text 16, 20, 21, 24 Y6 T1 Text 13, 15, 16	Writing: Functional writing and Knowledge about language – Level C/D/E Reading: Reading for information and Awareness of genre – Level C/D/E	AT2 Reading – Level 3/4/5 AT3 Writing – Level 3/4/5
page 116	The crazy boat race	To write a newspaper report about a picture.	Remind children to use journalistic features when writing their newspaper report.	Y4 T1 Text 16, 20, 21, 24 Y6 T1 Text 13, 15, 16	Writing: Functional writing and Knowledge about language – Level C/D/E Reading: Reading for information and Awareness of genre – Level C/D/E	AT2 Reading – Level 3/4/5 AT3 Writing – Level 3/4/5

Page	Activity	Objective	Teachers' notes	National Literacy Strategy links	Scottish Curriculum links	KS2 Levels
page 117	Newspaper headlines	To write headlines and news articles.	This activity can be used as an assessment or consolidation sheet on writing effective newspaper headlines and articles.	Y4 T1 Text 16, 20, 21, 24 Y6 T1 Text 13, 15, 16	Writing: Functional writing and Knowledge about language – Level D/E Reading: Reading for information and Awareness of genre – Level D/E	AT2 Reading – Level 4/5 AT3 Writing – Level 4/5
page 118	Water travel	To make notes and write an explanatory text about a form of water travel.	This activity requires children to make a list and then produce an explanatory text on water travel.	Y4 T2 Text 20, 25	Writing: Functional writing and Knowledge about language – Level D/E Reading: Reading for information and Awareness of genre – Level D/E	AT2 Reading – Level 3/4/5 AT3 Writing – Level 3/4/5
page 119	Cross-section through the Earth	To write a short piece of information from a labelled diagram.	Let children look at examples of encyclopaedia entries as writing models. Check that children look at the diagram carefully. Children need to be able to both interpret a diagram and produce relevant diagrams.	Y6 T1 Text 13, 17	Writing: Functional writing and Knowledge about language – Level D/E Reading: Reading for information and Awareness of genre – Level D/E	AT2 Reading – Level 4/5 AT3 Writing – Level 4/5
page 120	The Arctic and the Antarctic	To write information paragraphs from notes in a chart.	This activity requires children to read and rearrange information from a chart and re-present it in a continuous narrative using paragraphs.	Y4 T2 Text 22	Writing: Functional writing and Knowledge about language – Level D/E Reading: Reading for information and Awareness of genre – Level D/E	AT2 Reading – Level 4/5 AT3 Writing – Level 4/5
page 121	The Hoot and Screech Club	To recognise features of persuasive writing.	The missing words are: fast; nesting; are; to; houses; if; came; the; set; barn; other; would; sure; the; supplying; over; place; help. Read together the completed sheet and discuss features of persuasive writing.	Y4 T3 Sentence 16	Writing: Functional writing and Knowledge about language – Level D/E Reading: Reading for information and Awareness of genre – Level D/E	AT2 Reading – Level 4/5 AT3 Writing – Level 4/5
page 122	Safari park poster	To design a poster that is easy to read and eye-catching.	Read the instructions and discuss children's ideas for making the poster easy to read and eye-catching.	Y4 T3 Text 18, 19, 25	Writing: Functional writing and Knowledge about language – Level D/E Reading: Reading for information and Awareness of genre – Level D/E	AT2 Reading – Level 3/4/5 AT3 Writing – Level 3/4/5
page 123	The amazing snowball machine	To design an advertisement using persuasive language.	Remind children to use language descriptively and persuasively.	Y4 T3 Text 18, 19, 25	Writing: Functional writing and Knowledge about language – Level D/E Reading: Reading for information and Awareness of genre – Level D/E	AT2 Reading – Level 4/5 AT3 Writing – Level 4/5
page 124	Safety rhymes	To compose a rhyme that conveys a safety message.	Talk about how 'I hear thunder' has a simple rhyming pattern that people can remember. Discuss ways to use this for the safety rhyme.	Y4 T3 Text 18, 19, 25	Writing: Functional writing and Knowledge about language – Level D/E Reading: Reading for information and Awareness of genre – Level D/E	AT2 Reading – Level 4/5 AT3 Writing – Level 4/5
page 125	Spanish Armada report	To use features and layout of reports to write a report of an event.	Before the activity, discuss what the English sailor might have seen and how the sheet helps plan out the children's ideas.	Y5 T1 Text 21, 23, 24, 26	Writing: Imaginative writing and Knowledge about language – Level D/E Reading: Reading for information and Awareness of genre – Level D/E	AT2 Reading – Level 4/5 AT3 Writing – Level 4/5
page 126	Police report	To recognise and write in the style of a police report.	Remind the children that police reports just describe the facts and do not use descriptive or figurative language.	Y5 T1 Text 21	Writing: Functional writing and Knowledge about language – Level D/E Reading: Reading for information and Awareness of genre – Level D/E	AT2 Reading – Level 4/5 AT3 Writing – Level 4/5
page 127	Zoos	To separate two sides of an argument about zoos and write their own opinion.	Explain that the children need to gather all the arguments of both sides before they can expect to argue a case well. Try to get children to add the opposing argument into their writing, but explain why the opposition have got it wrong'.	Y4 T3 Text 16, 17 Y6 T2 Text 15, 16, 18, 19	Writing: Personal writing and Knowledge about language – Level D/E Reading: Reading for information and Awareness of genre – Level D/E	AT2 Reading – Level 4/5 AT3 Writing – Level 4/5

SCHOLASTIC
www.scholastic.co.uk

Muddled names

The muddled names below belong to well-known story characters.

✦ Unmuddle them using the clues to help.

Clues

- D I E P P P R E I _____ (rats)

- G A M R H C I N _____ (prince)

- D I N A L A D _____ (sesame)

- L E E R D I N C A L _____ (slipper)

- W N S O E H I T W _____ (7)

- E D R G N I D I R D O H O _____ (wolf)

✦ Here are some more jumbled names of famous characters for you to work out.

- N O I R B O O D H _____ (Sherwood)

- M O T T B U H M _____ (small man)

- N G K I R R T H A U _____ (round table)

✦ Choose one character from a fairy story and write the story from their point of view, for example 'One day I was cleaning the grate when I ...'

Opposites

There are lots of prefixes you can put at the front of words to change them into their opposites. There's **in-** and **im-** and **ir-** and **il-**.

♣ Which prefix would fit these words?

accurate

capable

considerate

credible

dependent

direct

legal

logical

polite

possible

probable

regular

♣ **in-** is probably the most popular prefix. List as many **in-** words as you can.

♣ Oh dear, all these words have been mixed up. It's up to you to put them right.

irmobile

imattentive

imcorrect

iladequate

unfinite

inperfect

irexpensive

ilresponsible

imconvenient

uncomplete

Number puzzles

unum means one in Latin.	**bi** means two.	**tri** means three.	**decem** means ten.
♣ Discuss with a friend what these words mean:	♣ Can you add to this list?	♣ Solve the clues to find words beginning with **tri–** that mean the following:	♣ See how many words beginning with **dec–** you can find. Take care – you want only those connected with ten!
unique	bilingual	a three-sided figure	December
uniform	bigamist	a three-wheeled bike	
unit		a three-legged stand	
unisex		a three-coloured flag	
union		a three-pronged fork	
unicorn		a three-people band	
united		a million, million, million	
unicycle		three children born together	
unify	♣ Check in your dictionary to make sure you know what all the words mean.		♣ On the back of this sheet write one calendar entry for each month of the year using a word from these lists every time.
universal			
♣ Check in your dictionary to see if you were right.			

Family trees

✤ Try these endings on the words below. Some will fit and some will not.

| -ward | -less | -ness | -ish | -ly | -ing | -ed | -ful |

| kind | slow | worth | life | home |

✤ Now use the endings to 'grow' word families. The first one has been done for you.

back

use

warm

hopeless

hopeful

hoped

hoping

hope

Become a tryer, thinker, writer...

✤ **Try** putting the suffix -er on to the ends of these words:

talk

work

help

drink

dream

listen

✤ **Think!** What kind of words do these verbs now become?

✤ **Write** down some of the -er words that describe you.
What am I?

a writer

_____

_____

_____

_____

Beware! Some letters (like n or p) double up before a suffix, like run → runner, skip → skipper.

✤ Check your -er words again!

No! Not me! I'm not a guzzler!
✤ Add a few more -er words that you don't like to be (or find difficult to be).

_____

_____

Shhh ...

❖ Finish these words with the silent letters opposite.

___reckage ___nit lis___en forei___n

___raith thou___ has___en ___nat

___riting ___night ___nome ___nee

sa___mon sa___ms qua___m

fas___en desi___n ___narled

nei___ bour cau___ ___t

Find **ten** words with silent letters hidden in this puzzle. Search across and down.

❖ Circle the words when you find them. One is done for you.

❖ How do people who cannot hear or speak communicate with each other?

T	C	W	R	A	P	P	E	D
A	O	R	T	O	K	S	O	E
W	R	I	T	E	N	A	U	S
R	P	T	I	T	O	L	G	I
Y	S	H	G	H	W	M	H	G
T	F	E	I	G	N	S	T	N

NO FUSS
PHOTOCOPIABLE

SCHOLASTIC
www.scholastic.co.uk

Speed trap

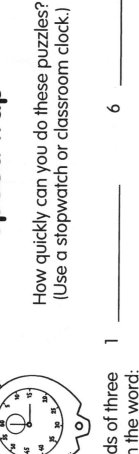

How quickly can you do these puzzles?
(Use a stopwatch or classroom clock.)

♣ Find twenty words of three
or more letters from the word:

grandiloquent

1 _____
2 _____
3 _____
4 _____
5 _____

6 _____
7 _____
8 _____
9 _____
10 _____

11 _____
12 _____
13 _____
14 _____
15 _____

16 _____
17 _____
18 _____
19 _____
20 _____

♣ How long did you take? _____

♣ Score your answers   3 points for a 3 letter word
5 points for a 4 letter word
7 points for a 5 letter word
8 points for any word over five letters.

♣ What does grandiloquent mean?
♣ Find more words which have a similar usage,
for example, **magnificent**. Try to find three.

I scored _____ points.

Instead of 'said'

♣ See how many different words you can use instead of 'said' to make this conversation sound more lively. Read the whole discussion before you start choosing your words. Then write them in the spaces provided.

We're going now!!

'Hurry up Harry!' said _____ Dad.

'What are you doing?' said _____ Dad. 'Hurry up, or you'll be late for school.'

'It's all right Dad,' said _____ Harry.

'No, it isn't' said _____ Dad. 'Here's your coat, put it on. We're going now.'

'Can we go by car?' said _____ Harry.

'No,' said _____ Dad. 'We're walking.' And so they set off for school.

'Mind that car,' said _____ Dad. 'Keep on the path.'

'Wait for me!' said _____ Harry as he lagged behind.

'I'm just going into the shop,' said _____ Harry.

'Oh no you're not,' said _____ Dad.

'Look, there's Ben,' said _____ Harry.

'Hi Ben,' he said _____ from across the street. They got through the school gate just in time.

'Bye-bye Harry,' said _____ Dad. The boys went in.

'Good morning,' Miss Jones said _____ to them.

SCHOLASTIC
www.scholastic.co.uk

Nice words

Here are some words for **nice**.
Can you find more in the thesaurus?

pleasant delightful agreeable enjoyable good lovely

✤ Choose a different word to replace **nice** each time it appears in the story below.

Saturday was a **nice** _____ day. We went to town to do

some shopping. The weather was **nice** _____. We had

some **nice** _____ ice-cream and a **nice** _____

walk round the shopping centre. I bought a **nice** _____

new scarf. Then we went home.

✤ Write about something you really enjoyed on the back of this sheet. Use as many different words as you can for **nice**.

Synonyms

Some words have similar meanings, for example,

I am ⟨ glad
        happy
        cheerful

✿ Find the **synonym** (similar) word hidden in the squashed-up letters below. Circle the word then write another synonym in the space beside it. The first one has been done for you.

- sly   D I S C R A F T Y I A B L E   artful _____

- dull   P R E F D O W D Y E D   _____

- aid   G R H E L P P D E R   _____

- shout   E R G B A W L I Z E   _____

- hug   C U D D L E P I N G   _____

- mop   S T E W I P E R S   _____

- ooze   O E F S W E E P G   _____

Hint: use a dictionary or word book to help find new words.

✿ Have you got a thesaurus in your school?
Find out how a thesaurus would help you with this puzzle.

Alphabetical order

✤ Put these lists into alphabetical order.

1 Look at the
   first letters.

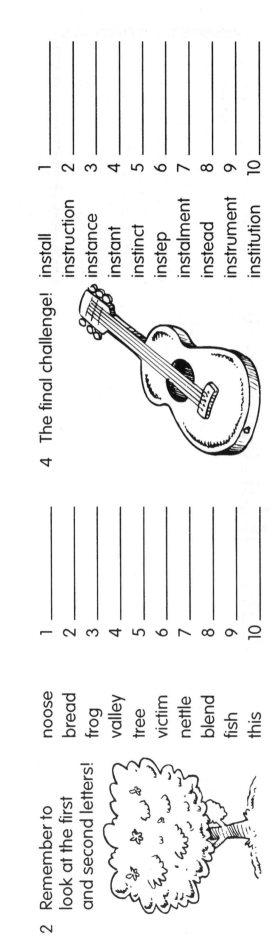

	zoo	1 ___
	when	2 ___
	mark	3 ___
	ghost	4 ___
	condense	5 ___
	abstract	6 ___
	under	7 ___
	star	8 ___
	egg	9 ___
	part	10 ___

2 Remember to
   look at the first
   and second letters!

	noose	1 ___
	bread	2 ___
	frog	3 ___
	valley	4 ___
	tree	5 ___
	victim	6 ___
	nettle	7 ___
	blend	8 ___
	fish	9 ___
	this	10 ___

3 This time look at
   the first, second
   and third letters.

	quite	1 ___
	cabbage	2 ___
	yell	3 ___
	hot	4 ___
	orange	5 ___
	yet	6 ___
	quack	7 ___
	house	8 ___
	card	9 ___
	ordinary	10 ___

4 The final challenge!

	install	1 ___
	instruction	2 ___
	instance	3 ___
	instant	4 ___
	instinct	5 ___
	instep	6 ___
	instalment	7 ___
	instead	8 ___
	instrument	9 ___
	institution	10 ___

A part-of-speech survey

What kinds of words are used most often?

Most dictionaries tell us what part of speech each listed word is: n. (noun) vb. (verb) adj. (adjective) and so on. Choose any page from your dictionary and rewrite the listed words in these columns (starting at the bottom!) See which column grows tallest!

adj. adjectives	**n.** nouns	**vb.** verbs	**adv.** adverbs	**others,** such as conj. pron. and so on

SCHOLASTIC
www.scholastic.co.uk

Close clues

These clues are for pairs of words which are close to each other in the dictionary.

● Fill in the missing words. The clues will help you to find them.

A fast aeroplane.

A woolly sweater.

j _____

j _____

A place where children go to learn.

A tool with two blades for cutting.

s _____

s _____

A machine people watch.

The bad mood someone is in.

t _____

t _____

Hair growing on a man's chin.

Any big animal.

b _____

b _____

A story that teaches people something.
A building where things are made
by machine.

f _____

f _____

● Make up a similar pair of clues yourself and try them on a friend.

_____

_____

_____

_____

Cracker word puzzles

Q When is a bucket unwell?
A When it is a little pail.

Homophones are words which sound the same but are spelt differently and have different meanings. Often jokes in Christmas crackers use homophones.

♣ Solve the clues below with one word, then match the word to its homophone. The first one is done for you:

flee ———————— bear

———————— break

———————— scull

———————— too

———————— flea

———————— pale

———————— coupe

———————— fore

———————— been

Clues:

1 to leave quickly

2 pirate's sign

3 to stop sharply

4 hen house

5 4

6 a Mexican jumping ————

7 a bucket

8 undressed

9 2

♣ Paint or draw a large Christmas cracker.
Write down three cracker riddles which use homophones.

Stepladders

A compound word is a word made by putting two words together.

❖ Go up and down the stepladders below using compound words or two-word phrases.

In this ladder every step must make a new word or phrase with the step above and the step below.

This stepladder goes one way only.

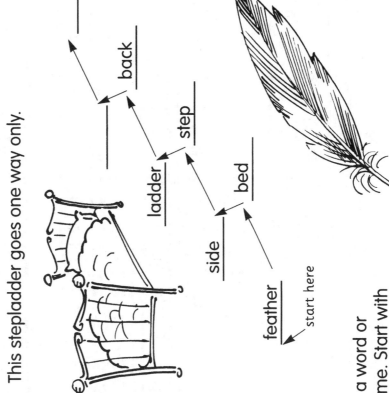

back

step

ladder

bed

side

feather
start here

ring

tale

fairy

boy

tall

cow
start here

❖ Play stepladders with a partner.
For example, you say 'snowball' and your partner must say a word or two-phrase word beginning with 'ball', for example, ball game. Start with five points each. If someone cannot make the next step he/she drops a point, and you must start again with a new word.

Word wall

This wall has bricks which need filling in.

❖ Find the word that finishes one word and starts the other. Use the words in the box below to help you build the wall.

For example: bit<u>ten</u>
<u>tenant</u>

	ten	ant
bit		

bit	ant		guinea	sty
shame	on			ship
way	let		tab	bit
bid		ounce		ate
pass	hole		bar	par	fully

den	out	ten	pig
kin	gain	or	don
port	less		

❖ Build your own word wall here.

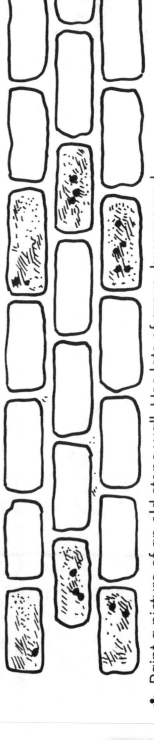

❖ Paint a picture of an old stone wall. Use lots of greys, browns and greens to show the mossy wall.

Seeing double

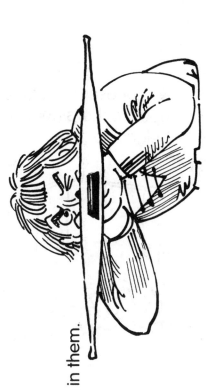

All these words have double letters:

- Moving very quickly – r u **n n** i n g
- To laugh in a high pitched voice – g i **g g** l e
- A seat on a bike – s a **d d** l e
- William Tell shot an arrow through one – a **p p** l e

❖ Fill in the missing letters below. Use the clues to help.

Clues

- Hit nails with it   __ __ m m __ __

- At the start   __ __ __ n n __ __

- The largest   __ __ g g __ __ __

- Meal in the evening   __ __ p p __ __

- Centre   __ __ __ d d __ __

- Moving in water   __ __ __ m m __ __

- A shoe worn indoors   __ __ p p __ __

❖ Write down as many words as you can think of with double letters in them.

❖ Who was William Tell?
Find out about him and the story about the apple.

Is it 'it's' or 'its'?

✣ Choose the right one to fill each space. Remember that 'it's' (with an apostrophe) stands for *it is* while 'its' (without an apostrophe) is to do with belonging.

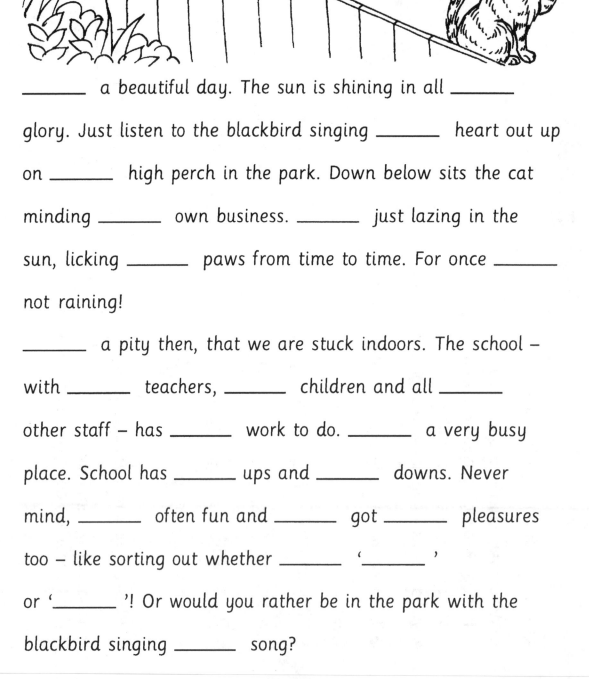

_____ a beautiful day. The sun is shining in all _____

glory. Just listen to the blackbird singing _____ heart out up

on _____ high perch in the park. Down below sits the cat

minding _____ own business. _____ just lazing in the

sun, licking _____ paws from time to time. For once _____

not raining!

_____ a pity then, that we are stuck indoors. The school –

with _____ teachers, _____ children and all _____

other staff – has _____ work to do. _____ a very busy

place. School has _____ ups and _____ downs. Never

mind, _____ often fun and _____ got _____ pleasures

too – like sorting out whether _____ ' _____ '

or ' _____ '! Or would you rather be in the park with the

blackbird singing _____ song?

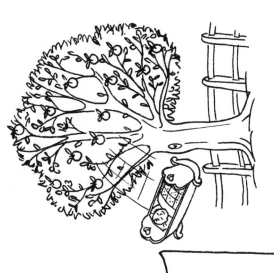

WPC Clough in action

Written below are some extracts from WPC Clough's diary, after she was called to the scene of an accident.

✿ Supply the vital missing words. (CLUE: they all contain the letter pattern **ough**.)

✿ Brainstorm all the words you can think of with **ough** in them first to help you.

Question 1 Have you always lived in _____, madam?

Question 2 Which _____ was it exactly that the cradle fell from?

Question 3 Was there not a _____ branch to put the cradle on?

Question 4 The neighbours tell me they heard the baby _____ and spluttering just before the incident. Is that so?

Question 5 Do you now believe you _____ to have stayed outside near the baby?

Question 6 Had the field been _____ recently? Yes? What a good job or the baby would have had a very _____ landing.

Well, that's _____ for now, thank you, madam. Make sure you take more care in future.

✿ Have you guessed which nursery rhyme this was based on?

✿ Choose a favourite rhyme and a different letter pattern and set up a similar interview to try out on a friend.

Doubling up

The two suffixes **-ing** and **-ed** are often used at the end of verbs.
They tell us what's happening today and what happened yesterday.
Sometimes when you add **-ing** or **-ed** to a word something doubles up.

♣ Look carefully at the words in the balloons. Add other words that have the same doubling up trick!

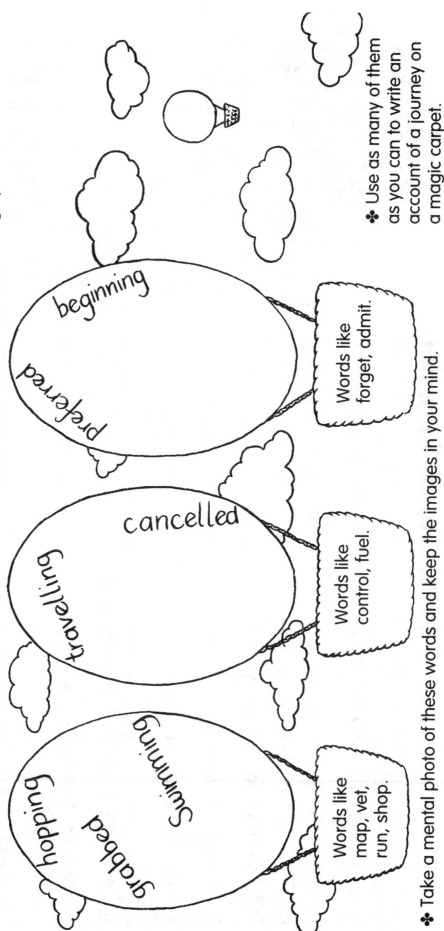

beginning

preferred

Words like
forget, admit.

cancelled

travelling

Words like
control, fuel.

hopping

grabbed

Swimming

Words like
map, vet,
run, shop.

♣ Use as many of them as you can to write an account of a journey on a magic carpet.

♣ Take a mental photo of these words and keep the images in your mind.

Night and day

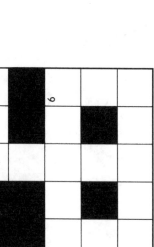

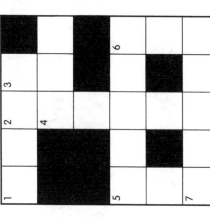

✤ Draw a line between opposites.

night	humble
closed	large
proud	war
retreat	day
peace	advance
small	open
seldom	often
slow	rapid

✤ Solve the crossword below by placing the opposite word to the clue in the boxes.

Across
1 first
4 bottom
5 quickens
7 day

Down
2 weak
3 from
5 moon
6 stand

We often use opposites in sayings, for example, 'through thick and thin', and 'it's an open and shut case'.

✤ Choose a saying with opposites in it and draw a picture to illustrate it. It can be funny or serious.

Homonyms

Q What jumper needs a rider?   **A** A polo neck jumper.

Some words **look** the same but have a different **sense** depending on their use, for example, pole.

• The **pole** marks the footpath.
• A **pole** is $5\frac{1}{2}$ yards in imperial measure.
• The North **Pole** is in the Arctic Circle.

✤ Find the **homonyms** which complete both sentences in each pair:

1 • Every _____ detail is considered.
   • There are sixty seconds in one _____

2 • This is a _____ long jump, which will win a medal.
   • You use a gramophone to play a _____.

3 • The bank is giving _____ on my savings.
   • My main _____ is music.

Here are eight more words which have different meanings depending upon their use.

score	cue	racket	left
light	nice	object	spring

✤ Design a crossword using some of these words and their different meanings. For example: **Q** Which is the bounciest time of the year? **A** Spring.

✤ Write down as many sayings and ways of using the word 'hand', for example: she is a handy person.

Name _____

Figures of speech

Sometimes we use phrases that don't quite say what they mean!

❖ Look at these pictures and you'll get the idea.

a storm in a teacup

a bee in her bonnet

hopping mad

❖ Now it's your turn. Draw a picture to illustrate the sayings below:

like a dog with two tails

a flea in your ear

blowing his own trumpet

❖ Discuss with your friend what these sayings really mean.
❖ Think of some more and illustrate them on a large sheet of paper.
❖ Mount a display of everyone's illustrations.

Name _____

Daily bread

♣ Fill the shelves in the baker's shop with drawings of these products which come from all over the world.

nans	scones	
buns	rolls	
bagels	chapatti	
blinis	croissants	
cottage loaf	ciabatta	
pitta	pikelet	
matzo	sourdough	
butties	tortilla	
pizza	soda farl	
granary	oatcake	
pumpernickel	stottycake	
baps	poppadom	
baguette	girdlescone	
puri		

♣ Add items from your local baker's.
♣ Check the origins of the words you don't know.

♣ Start collecting bread recipes in a class book.

NO FUSS
PHOTOCOPIABLE

Word origins

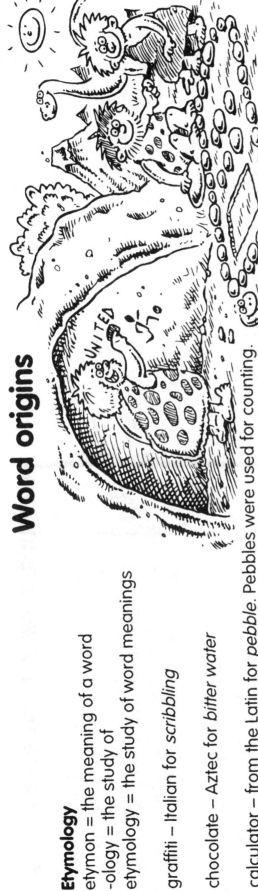

Etymology
etymon = the meaning of a word
-ology = the study of
etymology = the study of word meanings

graffiti – Italian for *scribbling*

chocolate – Aztec for *bitter water*

calculator – from the Latin for *pebble*. Pebbles were used for counting.

❧ Find the origins of these words:

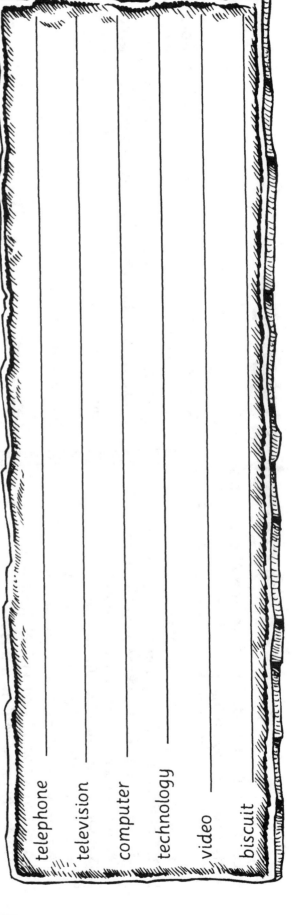

telephone

television

computer

technology

video

biscuit

A changing language

✤ Look carefully at these lines from 'The Wife of Bath's Tale' written by Geoffrey Chaucer:

I grante thee lyf, if thou kanst tellen me
What thing is it that wommen moost desiren.
Be war, and keep thy nekke-boon from iren!
And if thou kanst nat tellen it anon,
Yet wol I yeve thee leve for to gon
A twelf-month and a day, to seche and leere
An answere suffisant in this mateere;
And suretee wol I han, er that thou pace,
Thy body for to yelden in this place.

This is what English was like 600 years ago! It has changed a lot since then and it keeps on changing all the time as we need new words and phrases for new situations.

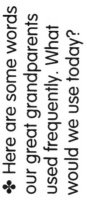

✤ Discuss Chaucer's English with a friend. What words do you recognise? How would we spell them today?

✤ See if you can work out what Chaucer is saying.

✤ Here are some words our great grandparents used frequently. What would we use today?

wireless →

gramophone →

petticoat →

stove →

gas mantle →

closet →

long johns →

toasting fork →

jerry →

drawers →

✤ Make a list of words we use today that our great grandparents would not have heard when they were young.

computer

astronaut

_____

_____

_____

_____

_____

_____

_____

_____

Proverbs

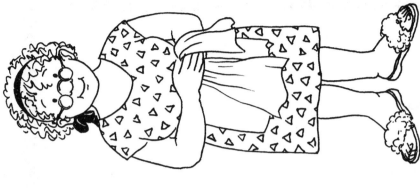

Grannies from the Caribbean are often full of good advice for their grandchildren.

♣ Write these Creole proverbs out in standard English.

• 'Dih older dih violin,
de sweeter de tune.'

_____

• 'Hurry hurry mek bad curry.'

_____

• 'When de farmer away,
Jackass take holiday.'

_____

• 'Better don't count de
chickens before dey hatch.'

_____

• 'Don' never hang yuh hat
higher dan yuh can reach.'

_____

• 'Who de cap fit
let dem wear it.'

_____

♣ Discuss with a friend
what advice these
proverbs are actually
giving.

♣ Make a collection of
useful proverbs for your
class.

Similes

Similes are a good way of describing things by comparing them with something else, by saying they are **like** or **as** something else. We use them all the time.

❖ When we use the same similes over and over again, they lose their power and become **clichés**. Now try the list again but think more carefully and make some more unusual comparisons.

as black as

as white as

as quick as

as blind as a

as strong as a

as weak as a

as clean as a

as cool as a

as bright as a

❖ Finish off these **similes** as fast as you can.

as black as _____

as white as _____

as quick as _____

as blind as a _____

as strong as a _____

as weak as a _____

as clean as a _____

as cool as a _____

as bright as a _____

❖ Write a description of a friend using similes.

Floorboards

❖ Flit across the floorboards using the four-step routine.

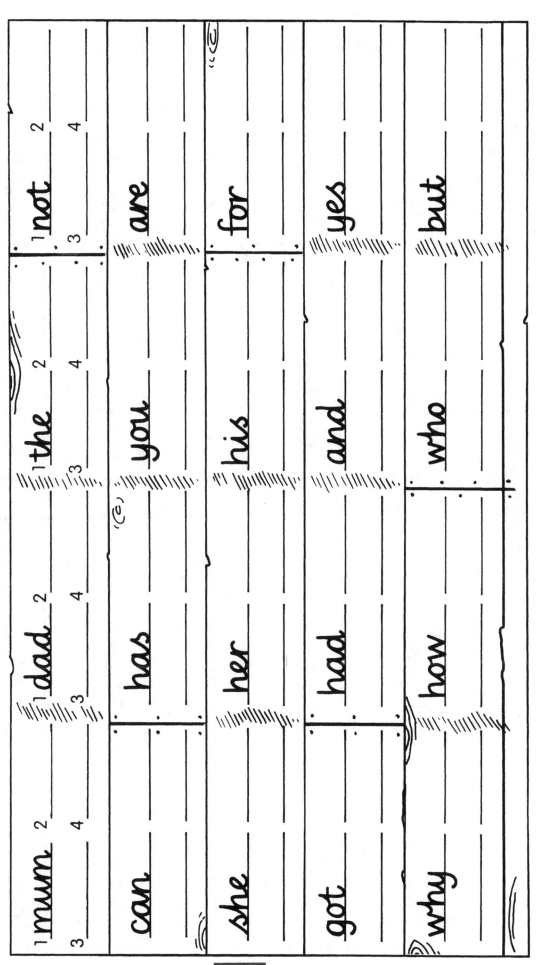

mum	dad	the	not
can	has	you	are
she	her	his	for
got	had	and	yes
why	how	who	but

Build a wall

❖ Build this brick wall using the four-step routine.

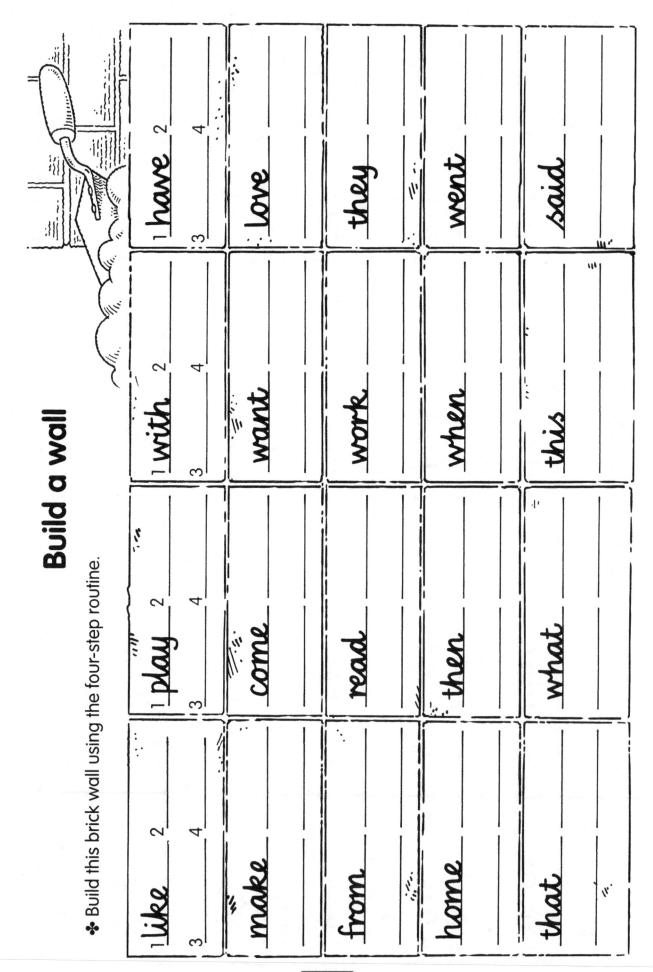

¹like ² ³ ⁴	¹play ² ³ ⁴	¹with ² ³ ⁴	¹have ² ³ ⁴
make	come	want	love
from	read	work	they
home	then	when	went
that	what	this	said

Hissing sounds

✿ Practise writing *ss* then use the four-step routine to fill in the spaces below.

1 *hiss*

2 _____

3 _____

4 _____

mess

toss

puss

Tessa

kiss

fussy

dress

less

class

✿ Do you know any more?

Bashful is...

ful ful ful ful ful ful ful ful

✿ Practise this letter pattern then fill in the speech bubbles with all the other words ending in **ful** that could describe Bashful.

I'm joyful and

careful and

dreadful and

watchful and

awful and

playful and

✿ Continue on the back of this sheet if you need to.

Name _____

A pony and trap ride

Mary is going on holiday to stay with an aunt and uncle whom she has never met. They live on the edge of a wild moor.

It was late at night when Mary _____ at the station and the

wind was howling. She _____ surprised to _____

that the remainder of her journey was by pony and trap.

Mary _____ up in the corner of the trap and

_____ her eyes on the road ahead. The lamps on the trap

_____ rays of light a little distance ahead. Mary

_____ fleeting glimpses of the things they passed.

They _____ through a tiny village and she

_____ whitewashed cottages and the lights of a public house.

They _____ an ancient church and a large vicarage. She

_____ the lights of a shop window. Then the village was gone.

At last the trotting horses _____ to go more slowly, as if

they _____ climbing a steep hill. She could see nothing now but

a wall of darkness on either side of the trap. She could _____

the panting of the horses. She leaned forward, the trap gave an enormous

jolt and lurched to a stop. They were there.

A wartime memory

I had to make sure that my brother was awake. He used to be very bad-tempered if he was disturbed in the night and he wanted to go back to sleep.

The Andersen shelter was dug into the ground. It had no heating and it always felt cold. My brother always used to grab the top bunk. There was often a puddle of rainwater on the rough cement floor.

If we heard the air-raid siren in the night we had to get up and put on warm clothes over our night things. We had to wear our shoes because it was often wet as we walked down the garden.

Mum used to hurry us down the garden path to the Andersen shelter. We weren't allowed to use a light so we often bumped into things. My dad was not with us. He was a soldier and we didn't even know where he was.

We could hear the planes going overhead and the thud of guns, but mum used to tell us not to worry. We would fall asleep and stay in the Andersen shelter until morning.

The twins, who were only babies, had to be put in the wicker laundry basket. They didn't even wake up. They had a stone hot-water bottle, wrapped in a blanket, to help keep them warm.

NO FUSS
PHOTOCOPIABLE

SCHOLASTIC
www.scholastic.co.uk

Direct speech

To help you	• Each time a character speaks start a new line. • Put speech marks at the beginning and end of words characters say.

✿ Write the words each character is saying inside speech marks.

Father Bear asked, '_____

'_____?'

'_____?' Baby Bear cried.

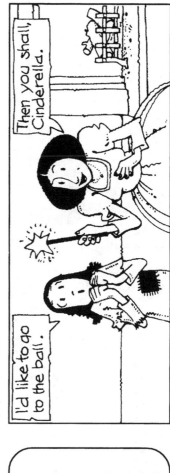

✿ Write a conversation between two characters in a story you know well. Set the conversation out using direct speech.

Direct and indirect

This is an example of **direct speech**: 'Hurry up, Liz,' said Harry.
Here is the same statement in **indirect speech**: Harry told Liz to hurry up.

✤ Look at the examples below.

✤ Link each piece of direct speech with the matching indirect speech.

'I'm fed up with this homework,' said Maxine.	Bill ordered Ryan to get his bike.
Karim thought it wasn't fair to blame the dog.	Maxine grumbled about her homework.
'Get your bike!' said Bill to Ryan.	'It's not fair to blame the dog,' said Karim.

✤ Rewrite this in *indirect* speech.

'It's the school trip today,' said Maxine.

'I don't want to go,' said Karim.

'Why not?' asked Bill.

'Because I've forgotton my lunch,' said Karim.

'Don't worry,' said Maxine. 'We'll give you some of ours.'

Shock horror game!

♣ Write or draw in some more dangers for this game. (The first one has been done for you.) Use exclamation marks to warn of the danger.

♣ Make up rules and play the game.

Danger! Snakes!

start

1 2 3 4 5 6 7 8 9 10 11

finish

Time to pause

Commas show you where to pause.

✤ Try to read this story without stopping.

Once upon a time there was a boy called Jack who lived with his mother who worked very hard but still she was very poor even though they had a large brown cow.

✤ Now read this.

Once upon a time there was a princess named Mary, who lived in a palace with her father, the King, who did not like to work, even though he had a lot of land to look after.

✤ Put some commas in the first story.

✤ Write a story for a friend to read aloud. Remember to put in the commas. (You can use the other side of the paper if you wish.)

Sophie and Jake find lost treasure.

Name _____

Agreeable verbs

What's wrong with this sentence?

The cakes is too hot to eat.

There are too many cakes for the verb 'is'!

The cakes *are* too hot to eat.

❖ Underline the verb that is wrong in each sentence.

❖ Rewrite the sentences using the correct form of the verb.

My cat have fleas. _____

The children likes playtime. _____

Wesley and Joe is singing. _____

Monster Mo wear huge boots. _____

The main road go past my house. _____

He ask too many questions. _____

Kate's big ed-venture

Kate has just learned the rule that adding -ed to verbs turns them into past actions, but sometimes she gets carried away!

♣ Can you correct her mistakes in this story?

Kate waked (............) very early, she getted (............) up quietly,

eated (............) her breakfast, goed (............) out, runned (............)

down the road and guess what she seed (............)? A big black horse

which she catched (............) hold of. She springed (............) up

on its back, holded (............) on tight and rided (............) away at

high speed. It taked (............) her a long way from home before she

falled (............) off. She finded (............) her way back and telled

(............) her parents. She sayed (............) she was sorry but still

she was sended (............) to bed and falled (............) fast asleep.

Story tenses

✤ Read the story extracts below.

Decide whether each is written in the past tense, eg. *Andrew stepped on to the plane. He sat down.* or in the present tense, eg. *Andrew steps on to the plane. He sits down.*

✤ Underline the words that helped you decide.

✤ Rewrite each extract using the opposite tense.

Using all of his strength Andrew leaped across the pit of snakes. He landed on the wet grass with a thud. Behind him the snakes hissed angrily.

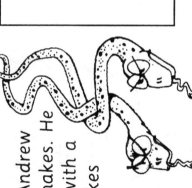

past	present

He reaches across and picks up the diamond. His heart is racing. It seems, for a moment, as if the diamond is going to slip from his grasp.

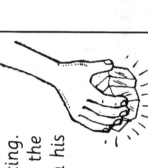

past	present

Funny faces

♣ Label each of these faces with a single word to describe how it looks to you. Look around the page for ideas!

♣ Now fill up this space by drawing and labelling some more faces.

proud	kind	tired
sleepy	weepy	ugly
mischievous	mysterious	pretty
hot	friendly	jolly
silly	hairy	happy
scared	wrinkly	clean
cheeky	angry	old
cold	cheerful	spotty
dirty	sad	cross
thin	plump	hungry
suspicious	worried	miserable

Messy, messier, messiest

❖ Draw a picture of the wettest day of the year.

❖ On the back of this sheet write about the messiest bedroom in the world.

❖ Fill in the table.

	messy	messier	messiest
red		redder	reddest
		hungrier	
sad		finer	wettest
jolly		bigger	
tame		smellier	
shiny			

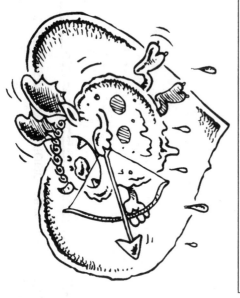

You're the most

✤ Read the poem below.

You're the most
You are like –
the juiciest jelly
the thickest milk shake
the fastest skateboard
the baggiest T-shirt
the brightest socks.

✤ Finish this poem.

A monster's valentine
You are like –
the slimiest slug
the spottiest toad

✤ Now write a 'You're the most' poem of your own.

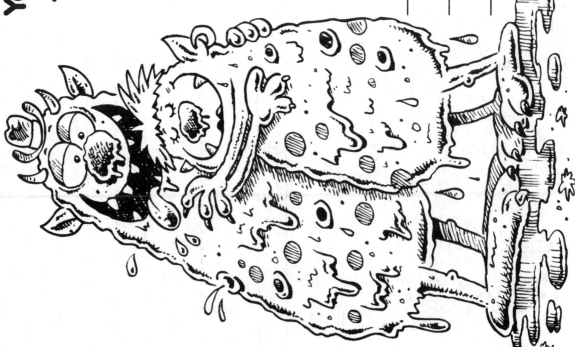

Two by two

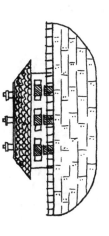

♣ Look at the pictures on the left. There is only one of everything. Help Noah to check his list to make sure he takes two of everything.

2 a _ _ _ _ _ _

2 b _ _ _ _ _ _

2 f _ _ _ _ _ _

2 m _ _ _ _ _ _

2 m _ _ _ _ _ _

2 w _ _ _ _ _ _

2 p _ _ _ _ _ _

2 w _ _ _ _ _ _

2 o _ _ _ _ _ _

2 m _ _ _ _ _ _

2 g _ _ _ _ _ _

a bag of c _ _ _ _ _ _

a box of m _ _ _ _ _ _

2 large b _ _ _ _ _ _

2 k _ _ _ _ _ _

2 s _ _ _ _ _ _

2 l _ _ _ _ _ _

2 kilos of p _ _ _ _ _ _

2 kilos of t _ _ _ _ _ _

2 pairs of s _ _ _ _ _ _

2 sets of b _ _ _ _ _ _

2 sets of d _ _ _ _ _ _

2 s _ _ _ _ _ _

♣ List the things you would take on the ark. You only have a small case. Justify your choice to a friend.

HAM'S WIFE · SPOON · LARGE BOX · MATCH · MOUSE · WOLF · OX · SHELF · BRUSH · TOMATO · GOOSE · CHERRY · FOX · ASS · DOMINO · LOAF · POTATO · KNIFE · MONKEY · PONY · BUFFALO · NOAH'S WIFE · MOSQUITO · SHOE

NO FUSS
PHOTOCOPIABLE

Collectomania

Often a collection of animals or things has a special word,
for example: **a swarm** of bees
a **herd** of elephants

✣ Solve the crossword below. The answers are all collective nouns.

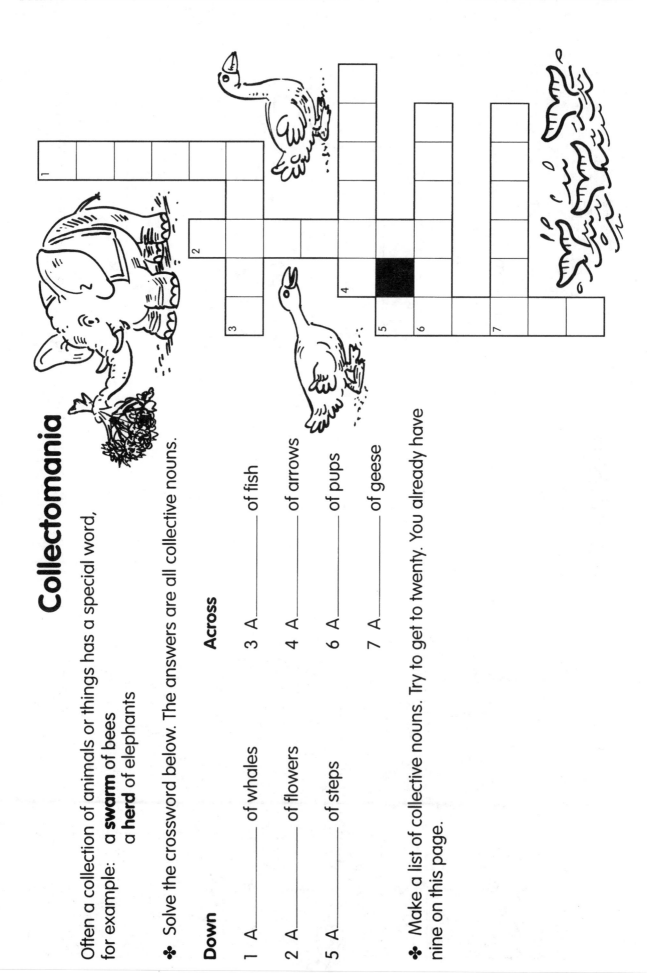

Down

1 A ——— of whales

2 A ——— of flowers

5 A ——— of steps

Across

3 A ——— of fish

4 A ——— of arrows

6 A ——— of pups

7 A ——— of geese

✣ Make a list of collective nouns. Try to get to twenty. You already have nine on this page.

Conjunctions

A conjunction is a joining word.

and   as   but   although   so   because

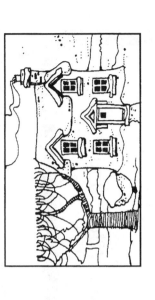
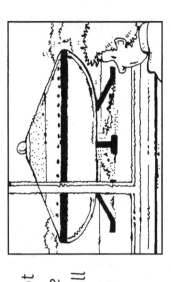

❖ Underline the conjunctions in this story opening:

It was a cold day and snow lay on the ground. Birds shivered in their nests because a chilling wind blew through the trees. Daylight arrived slowly as the sun rose lazily. There was no sign of human life although trails of smoke rose from many of the chimney pots.

❖ Add conjunctions to this story opening:

The pupils in Class 4 were all working very hard _____ they did not notice the spaceship land. At first no one was aware of it _____ the metal dome came to rest just outside the classroom window. Suddenly, all 24 pairs of eyes looked up in unison _____ there was a deafening noise. The door of the spaceship opened slowly _____ three purple aliens appeared.

❖ Choose one of the story openings above and rewrite it on a separate sheet. Miss out each conjunction and put a full stop in its place. Start the next word with a capital letter. Then read the story opening with and without the conjunctions. Write down which you think works best and say why.

NO FUSS
PHOTOCOPIABLE

Finding personal pronouns

✿ Can you improve this piece of writing by replacing most of the repeated names with personal pronouns? The first few lines have been done for you.

John and Jenny

John and Jenny were best friends. ~~John~~ He always went around with ~~Jenny~~ her, and
~~Jenny~~ she never left ~~John~~ him. ~~John and Jenny~~ They loved just playing and chatting endlessly.

'Do Jenny like that music?' John would say.

'Jenny think it's brilliant,' Jenny would reply.

'Did John finish your crisps? Give some to Jenny!' Jenny would cry.

'John have none left,' John would say sadly.

'What shall Jenny and John do now?' Jenny and John would often wonder.

'Let's hide so that no one will find Jenny and John.'

So that is what Jenny and John did, both of Jenny and John. Jenny and John would then disappear for hours.

You should have found that there are eleven different basic personal pronouns.

✿ Write each one again in these boxes.

Underlining adverbs

The underlined words in this story are adverbs.

When the monster rose up <u>angrily</u> from the

canal we were very scared. We ran <u>quickly</u>

to the police station and all started shouting

<u>excitedly</u>.

✤ Continue the story above and on the back of this sheet if you wish.

✤ Underline the adverbs you have used.

✤ Draw a picture of your story on the back of this sheet.

Tremendously revealing comments

✤ Use some of the adverbs and adjectives from this page, or any others you can think of, to express how you feel about the following things.

My friends are _____ .

My family is _____ .

My street is _____ .

My class is _____ .

My work is _____ .

My appearance is _____ .

My behaviour is _____ .

The weather is _____ .

The world is _____ .

What a _____ day!

absolutely   slightly
incredibly   extremely
strangely   occasionally
always   totally
quite   hysterically
hardly   extraordinary
calm   dull
exciting   enjoyable
interesting   disappointing
surprising   ghastly
infuriating   wonderful
funny   happy
clever   rude

Name _____

Holiday at sea

John and Wendy climbed down the steps into the noisy and bustling harbour. The sun shone brightly and there wasn't a cloud in the sky.

This was the first day of their first ever sailing holiday. They grinned at each other. They were excited. The luggage had to be stowed _____ in the cabin because there wasn't much room. It wasn't a very big boat. The wind was blowing _____ and they could feel the boat moving _____ against the harbour wall.

The children had been told they could go down to the beach for a swim. They _____ put on their swimming costumes, left the boat and ran _____ to the nearby beach.

John looked at the waves, rolling _____ down the beach. He shouted _____ to Wendy and jumped _____ into the waves. They were so strong that he struggled to keep his balance. Then Wendy ran into the sea and, holding John's hand, they jumped _____ in the waves.

Eventually the sun went in. John began to shiver _____ and they both grabbed their towels. They clambered _____ back to the boat.

Dinner was ready. Tomorrow they would set sail. Then, the holiday would really begin!

Spot the apostrophes

❖ Put in the apostrophes.

The monkeys tail

The dogs bone

The girls pencils

♣ Look at these unusual ones.

The children's chocolate
The fairy's wands
The fairies' wands

The monkeys tails

The dogs bone

The girls pencils

♣ Now put the apostrophes in these.

The babys nappies
The babies nappies
The ladys shoe
The ladies shoe

Can you spot the difference?

The pirate's treasure.

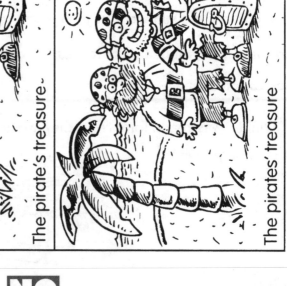

The pirates' treasure

The **apostrophe** is at the end here because there is more than one pirate.

SCHOLASTIC
www.scholastic.co.uk

Apostrophes

For informal pieces of writing, we often abbreviate. This means that words are shortened by popping in an apostrophe (') to show that there's a letter missing.

It's always happening to:

| is | – | 's |

How's that!
Who's there?
What's it like?

and to

| are | – | 're |

They're off!
We're late!
You're kidding!

and to

| not | – | n't |

I haven't – I mustn't
I can't – I oughtn't
I don't – I didn't
I daren't – I shouldn't
I won't – I couldn't
I mightn't – I wouldn't

✤ Use some of these to write a humorous poem about yourself.

In trouble again!

What's the big idea?

The sentence below has a **main clause** and a **subordinate clause.**

The boy I saw yesterday has a pony.

Main clause: **Subordinate clause:**
The boy has a pony.   I saw yesterday.

'The boy has a pony' is the main thing that you are being told. It's the **big idea.**

'I saw yesterday' tells you something less important about the boy. It's the **smaller idea.**

❖ Now look at these:

The chocolate that you gave me was very good.
The pig that can do tricks is in a film.
The clock that doesn't go is on the shelf.
The fish I bought on Saturday is striped.

♣ Write each main clause here:

♣ Make up some more sentences of your own like the ones above.

❖ Continue on the back of this sheet, if you wish.

NO FUSS
PHOTOCOPIABLE

SCHOLASTIC
www.scholastic.co.uk

Put them together

✤ Join each main clause with one subordinate clause to make a complete sentence.

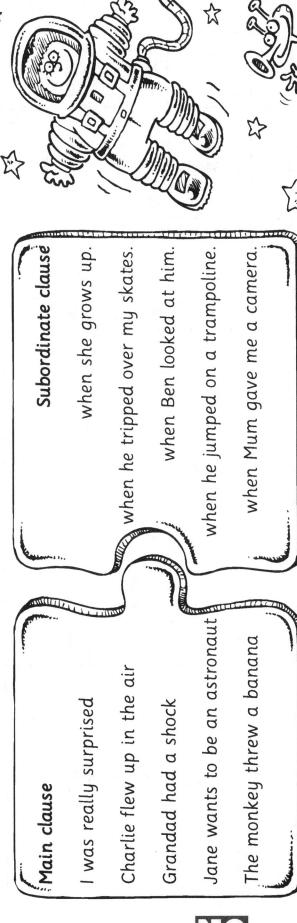

Subordinate clause

when she grows up.

when he tripped over my skates.

when Ben looked at him.

when he jumped on a trampoline.

when Mum gave me a camera.

Main clause

I was really surprised

Charlie flew up in the air

Grandad had a shock

Jane wants to be an astronaut

The monkey threw a banana

✤ Make up two sentences of your own:

when

when

Pick and mix

✤ Cut out the cards.

✤ Use them to make different sentences.

Some of your sentences will sound funny!

The	tasty	sausage	sizzled	scrumptiously
article (art)	adjective (adj)	noun (n)	verb (v)	adverb (adv)

(art) A	(art) A	(v) barked	(v) crashed	(adv) quickly
(adj) tiny	(adj) wobbly	(v) sizzled	(v) sailed	(adv) slowly
(n) dog	(n) mouse	(v) jumped	(adv) loudly	(adv) scrumptiously
(n) tiger	(n) ship	(v) squeaked	(adv) softly	(adv) happily

(art) The	(art) The
(adj) fluffy	(adj) striped
(adj) tasty	(adj) big

✤ Play a game like 'Happy Families' with a friend.

✤ Ask each other for the cards you need to make your sentences.

NO FUSS
PHOTOCOPIABLE

Sentencestics

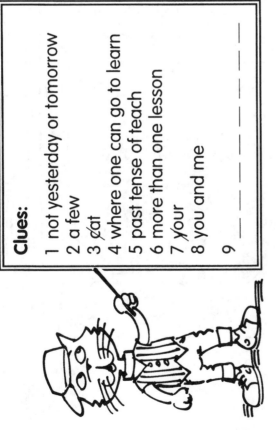

Clues:

1 not yesterday or tomorrow
2 a few
3 ¢at
4 where one can go to learn
5 past tense of teach
6 more than one lesson
7 ¥our
8 you and me
9 _ _ _ _ _ _ _ _ _

You now have nine words.

❖ Put them together to make a sentence. There are different combinations which make sense. Remember a sentence starts with a capital letter and ends with a full stop.

❖ Write a sentence about your favourite game. Put it into an acrostic form. You may have to change words so that it will make an acrostic. Write clues and ask a friend to solve it.

Banana split

Kim has asked her friend Dina how to make banana splits.

Dina:
'Well, you get a banana and cut it – you cut it the long way and you have to have a long dish to put it in. Then you put scoops of ice-cream between the two bits of banana – and then you can put cherries on top and pour on cream or chocolate sauce.'

Kim:
'I can't remember all that. Will you write out the recipe for me?'

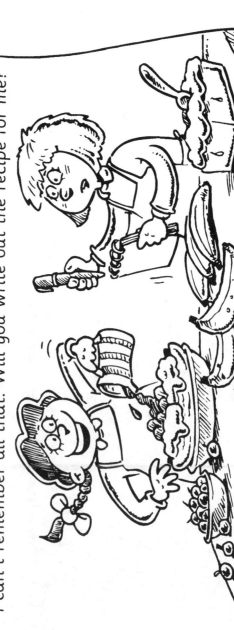

✤ Write out the recipe for banana split.

Remember that you just need to write out the important facts.

NO FUSS PHOTOCOPIABLE

SCHOLASTIC
www.scholastic.co.uk

Which way is it?

♣ Can you give Anwar directions to get from home to school?

1 Out of the house _____

2 Down _____

3 _____

4 _____

5 _____

6 _____

7 _____

8 _____

9 _____

10 _____

Is it down, up, under, over, right, left, past, straight on, along, across, beside, through, in, on or out?

SCHOOL

SCHOOL ROAD

Right

TREE AVENUE

PUB

railway bridge

left

TRAFFIC LIGHTS

SHOPS

CROSSROADS

BRIDGE

RIVER

ANWAR'S HOME

LONG HILL

MAIN ROAD

Put it where?

♣ Read the instructions, then draw these things in the right place.

Put the elephant in the deck-chair.

Put the sun-glasses on the elephant.

Put the sun-hat under the table.

Put the sausage in the sun-hat.

Put the jelly on top of the sausage.

Put the ice-cream at the end of the elephant's trunk.

Aircraft story

Imagine that you are the passenger in an aeroplane when the pilot collapses.
♣ Write the dialogue between you and the airport control tower.

ME   Help, the pilot has collapsed!
AIRPORT   Don't panic! What is your altitude?
ME   Um, 12 000 metres, I think.
AIRPORT

Aircraft language

altitude –
how high up you are

rudder –
needed to steer

wing flap –
needed to land

control tower

runway

throttle – makes
the plane go
faster and
slower

Let's talk!

Write your conversation here.

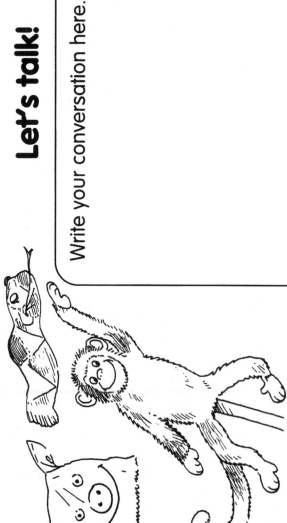

✤ Here are some simple handmade puppets. Write a conversation between two puppets. It could be between two of these puppets or two of your own.

✤ Make your puppets and use them to act out the conversation to the other children in your class.

SCHOLASTIC
www.scholastic.co.uk

Paragraphs

Paragraphs help you to organise your writing into sections.

♣ Decide how to organise this story opening into sections. Put // when:

- the story starts
- the time changes
- the place changes

♣ Continue the story, using paragraphs to organise your writing.
To show you are starting a new paragraph:

- start a new line
- indent your writing

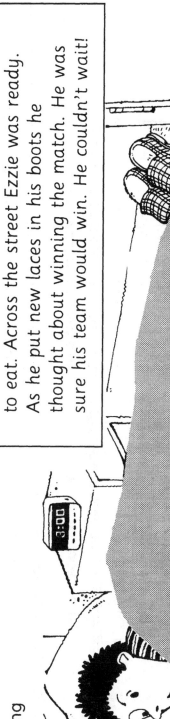

It was the morning of the big game. James snuggled into the warmth of his duvet, thinking nervously about the day ahead of him. At 8 o'clock his alarm rang. He sighed. This meant he had to get up. He flung back the duvet and eased his feet into his slippers. Finally he made his way across the room. In the kitchen his dad was cooking breakfast. James knew his dad was only trying to help, but he felt too sick to eat. Across the street Ezzie was ready. As he put new laces in his boots he thought about winning the match. He was sure his team would win. He couldn't wait!

Which person?

Ben could not stop laughing. Tears were pouring down his cheeks.

3rd person narrative

I could not stop laughing. Tears were pouring down my cheeks.

1st person narrative

✤ Decide whether these story openings are told in the first or third person. Tick the correct box.

I heard every word he said from my hiding place.

☐ 1st person narrative ☐ 3rd person narrative

The doorbell rang. Mike ignored it. The bell rang again. Mike sighed and stopped playing the game on his computer. 'This had better be important!' he muttered.

☐ 1st person narrative ☐ 3rd person narrative

Leah stormed through the doorway. She stopped in front of the sofa and glowered angrily at her brother.

☐ 1st person narrative ☐ 3rd person narrative

I guess it was just one of those things. I know I shouldn't really have lost my temper.

☐ 1st person narrative ☐ 3rd person narrative

They were all laughing, laughing at her.

☐ 1st person narrative ☐ 3rd person narrative

✿ Choose one story opening written in the third person. Rewrite the opening in the first person and continue the story.

Name _____

Ordering chapter headings

The chapter headings below tell the story of Damian Mill and his Formula 1 race for the world championship.

✤ Reorder the chapter headings to tell Damian's story from start to finish.

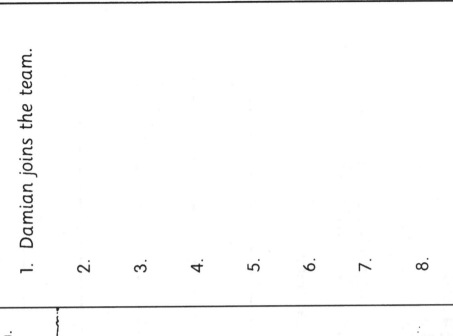

1. Damian joins the team.
2.
3.
4.
5.
6.
7.
8.

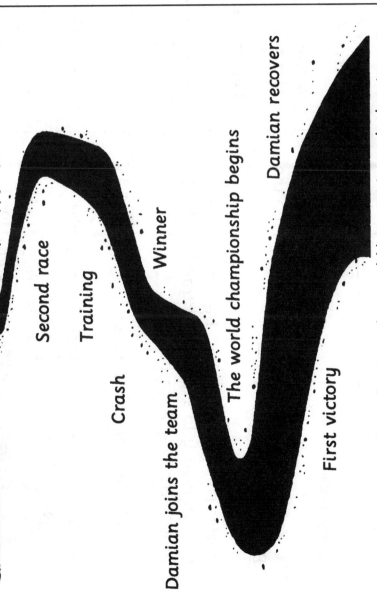

Second race

Training

Winner

Crash

Damian joins the team

The world championship begins

Damian recovers

First victory

✤ Write a paragraph explaining what could happen in each chapter.

Writing chapter headings

✦ Read the story outline.

✦ Write six chapter headings to explain what happens in each chapter.

Chapter headings

1. _____

2. _____

3. _____

4. _____

5. _____

6. _____

✦ Think of alternative chapter headings for each chapter.

Story outline

1. Zoë wants to play tennis. She gets into the British team.

2. Her parents realise that they don't have enough money to support her training. A local firm offers to sponsor her.

3. Zoë wins her first big match.

4. During her second match Zoë collapses.

5. Doctors are sure she'll never play tennis again. A new treatment is found.

6. Zoë recovers, retrains and goes on to win the British championship for the under 15s.

Name _____

The message

Imagine you are the commander of a spaceship. As you and your crew are passing a planet a message appears on your ship's screen.

♣ Use the key below to help you write down the first two words of the message in English on the screen.

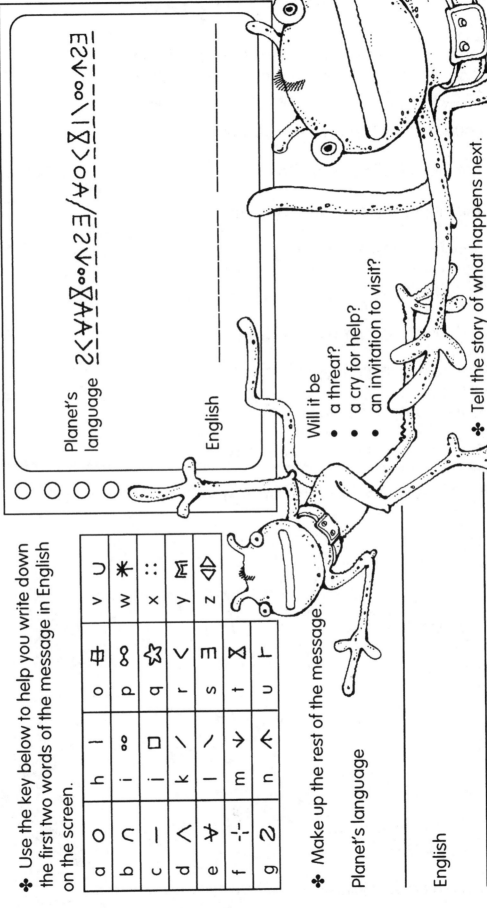

Planet's language

English

Will it be
- a threat?
- a cry for help?
- an invitation to visit?

✤ Tell the story of what happens next.

a	O	h	ʇ	o	⊕	v	∪
b	∪	i	∞̈	p	∞̊	w	✳
c	I	j	□	q	☆	x	∷
d	∨	k	╱	r	∨	y	∑
e	⋏	l	╱	s	ⴹ	z	�
f	∹	m	→	t	⋈		
g	⋜	n	←	u	⊤		

♣ Make up the rest of the message.

Planet's language

_____

English

_____

NO FUSS PHOTOCOPIABLE

ENGLISH AGES 7-11   **81**

Fun with puns

❖ Can you see the joke in these made-up book titles?
They all depend on **puns** – words that sound the same but
mean different things. Fill in the other meanings.

'Road Hog' by Laurie Dryver... (lorry driver)

'The Steep Cliff' by Eileen Dover... (_ _____ ____)

'The Haunted House' by Hugo First... (___ __ _____)

'Pray for me' by Neil Downe... (_____ ____)

'Keep Fit' by Jim Nastics... (_____)

'Keep it up' by Lucy Lastic... (_____ _____)

'Victorian Transport' by Orson Kart... (_____ ___ ____)

'Open House' by Colin Ennityme... (____ __ _____)

'The Treasure Chest' by Anne Teaks... (_____)

'Frank Conquers the World' by Betty Duzzant... (___ __ _____ ' _)

❖ Make a book of jokes with your friends based on puns.

Palindromes: ← this way, that way → ← either way →

A **palindrome** is a word that is spelt the same if you read the letters backwards or forwards.
For example, mum and dad are palindromic words.

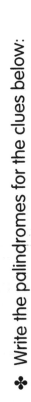

♣ Write the palindromes for the clues below:

Clues	Answer
1 12 o'clock mid-day.	— — —
2 A female sheep.	— — —
3 Invisible rays used for tracking objects.	— — —
4 Fizzy drink.	— — —

Clues	Answer
5 A religious sister.	— — —
6 A boat used by Inuit people.	— — —
7 The evening or day before.	— — —
8 A small seed in an apple.	— — —

♣ Who is the first woman to appear in the Bible?

♣ Find five more names of people which are palindromic.
(You already have several on this page.)

♣ Guess who?

● My first is first in the alphabet.
● My second is one more than half way in the alphabet.
● I am palindromic and have four letters.

● What is my name? — — — —

SCARY ALLITERATION

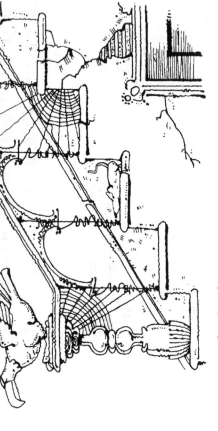

Alliteration is when words that are next to or near each other start with the same letter.

For example: black bat or sinister shape.

✤ Match up these words to make alliterations.

- whispering   spider
- spooky   wind
- fearful   castle
- creepy   fog

✤ Think of scary words to describe these objects. The words should start with the same letter.

Describing word	Object
squeaky	staircase
	mist
	night
	church
	tree

✤ Write a description of a scary place, using alliteration.

A rhyming puzzle

Words which rhyme sound the same at the end, for example,

{ pot
  knot }

However, they do not have to be spelled in the same way, for example,

{ done
  fun }

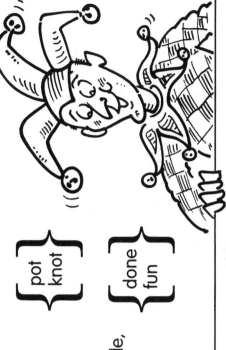

✿ Join the rhyming pairs below.
Be careful, there are some 'joker' words which do not match.
(There are seven rhyming pairs.)
Rearrange the 'joker' words to make a sentence.

sale		mouse		change
				care
	house			
			feet	flew
noose		seat		
	the		might	
you	hair			
		goose		
high			today	
pail				
weather		die		

_____

_____

_____

Remember, the sentence can be written in different ways.

✿ Write a poem about the weather that you can see out of the window today. Remember poems do not have to rhyme.

My farm-i-o!

Chorus:
There are dogs and cats and fleas and flies,
And they all live on my farm-i-o.
Elephants, ants, hippopotami too;
Everyone thinks I'm barmy-o!

Verse 1
I love my dogs. I love my cats.
I even love my vampire bats.
I've horses too, and
Butterflies blue,
And they all live on my farm-i-o.

Verse 2

Verse 3

❖ These are the chorus and first verse of a very silly song! Make up verses 2 and 3. Do a rough draft first. Then, when you are happy with it, neatly copy out the words here.

The thrushes' nest

(This poem, by John Clare, was written over a hundred years ago.)

Within a thick and spreading hawthorn bush
That overhung a molehill large and round,

How true she warped the moss to form a nest,
And modelled it with in the wood and clay;

I heard from morn to morn a merry thrush
Sing hymns to sunrise, and I drank the sound.

A brood of nature's minstrels chirp and fly
Glad as that sunshine and the laughing sky.

Ink spotted over shells of greeny blue;
And there I witnessed, in the sunny hours,

With joy; and, often an intruding guest,
I watched her secret toils from day to day –

And by and by, like heath bells gilt with dew,
There lay her shining eggs, as bright as flowers,

Like a volcano

♣ Write a poem on this volcano describing someone (yourself, maybe) in a rage.
Use some of the erupting words to help you, and continue on extra paper, if you wish.

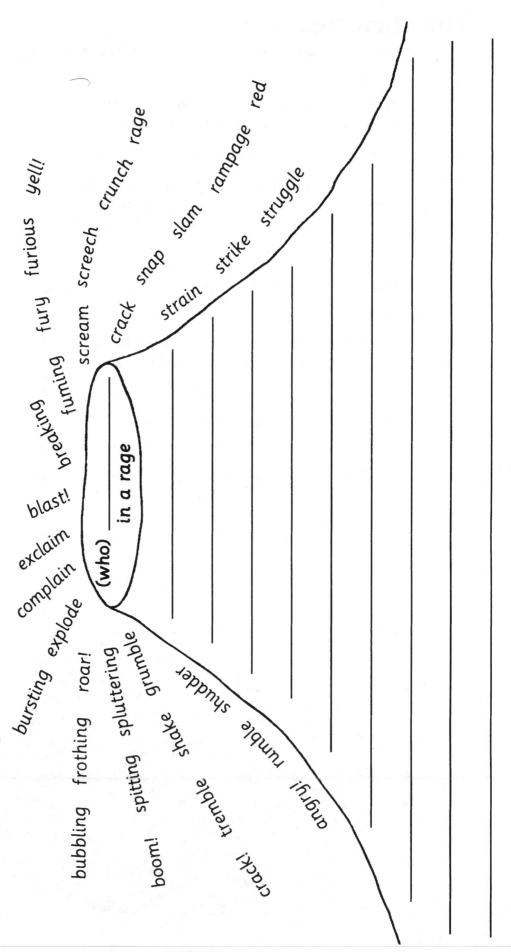

red
rampage
crunch rage
slam
screech
snap
strike struggle
scream
strain
crack
fuming
fury furious yell!
breaking
blast!
exclaim
complain
(who)
in a rage
bursting explode
roar!
spluttering
frothing
grumble
bubbling
spitting
shake
boom!
tremble
crack!
rumble shudder
angry!

NO
FUSS
PHOTOCOPIABLE

SCHOLASTIC
www.scholastic.co.uk

Name _____

Like a beautiful bird

❖ Fold this page along the centre fold. Cut out your bird. Fold again, and lift the wings.

❖ Now imagine flying like a bird.
Do you soar, hover, dive, glide, flutter, swerve or fall?

Centre fold

❖ Write a few lines along the feathers to describe yourself up there – and what you are seeing, thinking and feeling.

❖ Colour the head, edges and tail. Hang your bird up with a thread.

Weather myth

A myth is a traditional story. It usually includes imaginary characters or creatures. Myths are sometimes used to explain natural events.

✤ Plan ideas for a myth which could be used to explain each of the following types of weather.

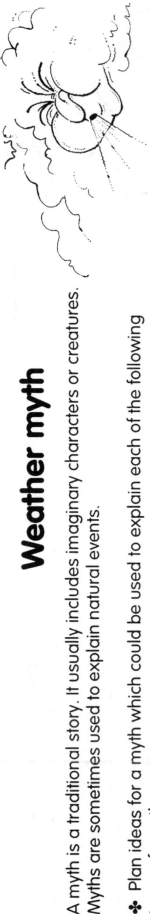

lightning

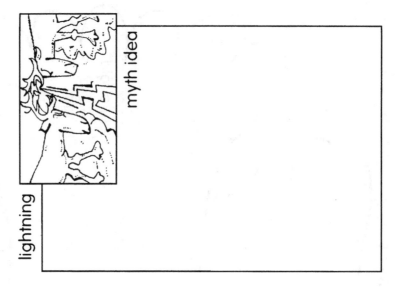

myth idea

sun

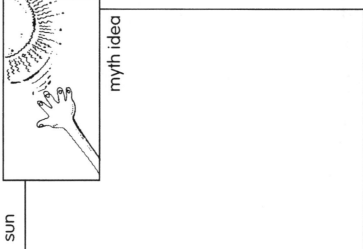

myth idea

rain

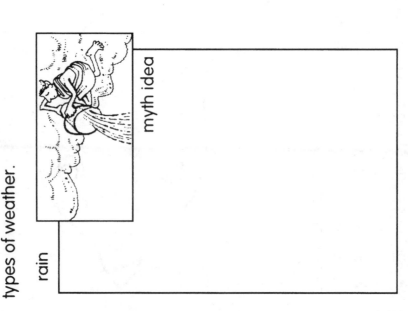

myth idea

✤ Write a weather myth.
Use one of the ideas you have outlined above or an idea of your choice.

A mixed-up myth

The computer bug has been at work and muddled this story.
❖ Work out the correct order and label the sentences **a** to **l** in order.

☐ ☐ ☐ a ☐ ☐ ☐

7 Narcissus wanted the person in the pool.

8 He looked in the water and saw a creature.

9 There was once a young man called Narcissus.

10 He looked at the reflection and forgot to eat and to sleep and so he died.

11 But the gods felt pity and changed him into a flower.

12 This was a punishment by the gods for his treatment of Echo.

☐ ☐ ☐ ☐ ☐ ☐

1 Narcissus did not love her.

2 Now the narcissus flower looks into the water and gazes at its own reflection.

3 Narcissus fell in love with his own reflection.

4 It happened that Narcissus was tired from hunting.

5 Echo, a nymph, loved him.

6 He rested by a pool of water.

❖ Find out what **narcissistic** means.

❖ Write the story of Narcissus and Echo in your own words. Make it interesting with lots of descriptive words.

Astronaut file

Imagine you are an astronaut who is applying to become the first person on Earth to journey to a newly discovered planet in outer space.

♣ Fill in the details about yourself on this astronaut-file application form.

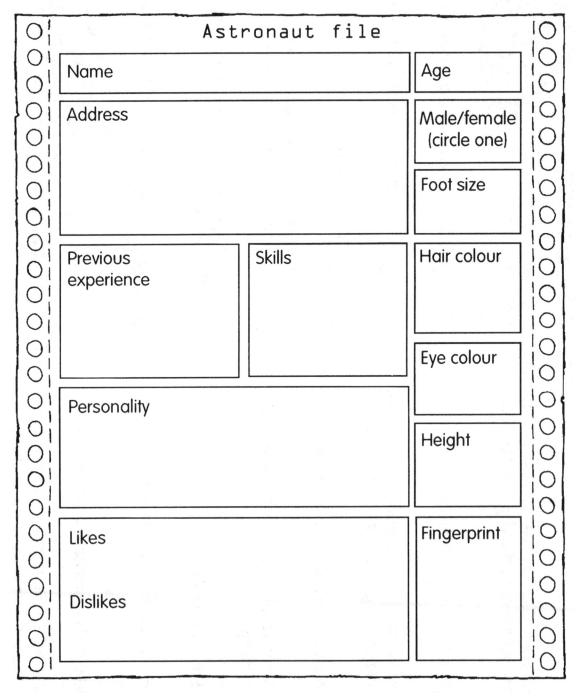

```
                        Astronaut file

  Name                                        Age

  Address                                     Male/female
                                              (circle one)

                                              Foot size

  Previous          Skills                    Hair colour
  experience

                                              Eye colour

  Personality
                                              Height

  Likes                                       Fingerprint


  Dislikes
```

♣ On the back of this sheet make a list of reasons why you think you are the best person for this job.

SCHOLASTIC
www.scholastic.co.uk

Characters in adventure stories

♣ List words which describe the behaviour and personalities of adventure story heroes/heroines and villains.

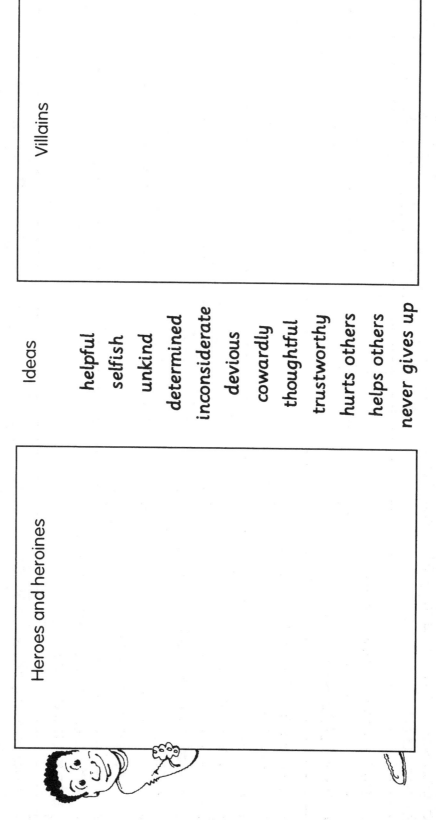

Villains

Ideas

helpful
selfish
unkind
determined
inconsiderate
devious
cowardly
thoughtful
trustworthy
hurts others
helps others
never gives up

Heroes and heroines

♣ Describe a hero/heroine and a villain from an adventure story you have read or seen. Write about their behaviour, personality and what they do.

Adventure story chart

✿ Choose one adventure story that you know.
Fill in the chart.

Name of the adventure story	Name of the hero or heroine	Describe the clothes the hero/heroine wears.	Name of the villain	Describe the clothes the villain wears.	Where is the story set?	Why does the hero/heroine set off on the adventure?	How does the adventure end?	Did you enjoy watching, listening to or reading the adventure story? Why?

NO FUSS
PHOTOCOPIABLE

Planet in danger story

♣ List the possible effects of each of these planetary problems.

Try to suggest one way in which each problem could be solved.

A strange disease breaks out

Effects

Solution

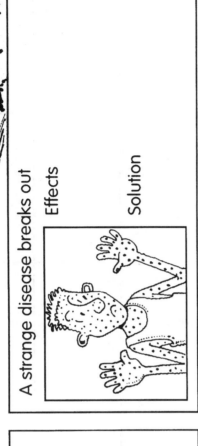

Attack by another planet

Effects

Solution

Food starts to run out

Effects

Solution

Poisonous fumes start to poison the air

Effects

Solution

♣ Write a story about a problem faced by beings on a planet. Describe what effects the problem causes and how the beings solve the problem.

Pollution

✤ Complete this chart. Use the last column for your own ideas.

Type of pollution	car fumes	litter	oil spills	cigarettes	
What causes it?					
What are its effects?					
Who can clean it?					
How can it be cleaned?					

✤ Choose one form of pollution and write a story about it.
Try to use adjectives to describe the pollution and its effects.

World War II diary

✿ Which person will you write your diary as? (tick)

☐ a soldier   ☐ a child in a city

☐ a nurse   ☐ an evacuee

☐ your idea _____

Date

Crime by numbers

✣ Roll a dice to find out which ingredients you will use in your story.

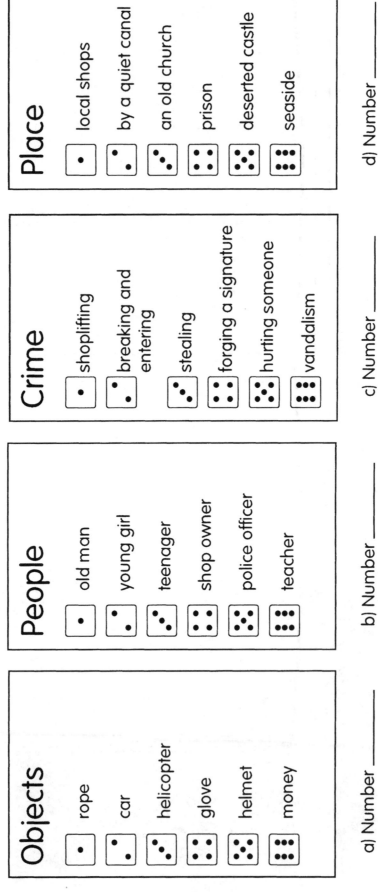

Objects

⚀	rope
⚁	car
⚂	helicopter
⚃	glove
⚄	helmet
⚅	money

People

⚀	old man
⚁	young girl
⚂	teenager
⚃	shop owner
⚄	police officer
⚅	teacher

Crime

⚀	shoplifting
⚁	breaking and entering
⚂	stealing
⚃	forging a signature
⚄	hurting someone
⚅	vandalism

Place

⚀	local shops
⚁	by a quiet canal
⚂	an old church
⚃	prison
⚄	deserted castle
⚅	seaside

a) Number _____
Object _____

b) Number _____
Person _____

c) Number _____
Crime _____

d) Number _____
Place _____

✣ Write your story using the ingredients you selected by rolling the dice.

Musical story

❧ Choose one of the following instruments.

other ——

❧ Complete the factfile below about the instrument you chose.

Ideas

• A young child is given the instrument as a present.

• The instrument is found in a garage by a family when they move into their new home.

• A child who wants to win a local music competition sees the instrument in a shop window.

• Your own idea.

Instrument factfile

The instrument plays (tick)

☐ high notes   ☐ low notes   ☐ softly

Which family of instruments does it belong to? (tick)

☐ brass   ☐ woodwind   ☐ string   ☐ other

How would someone play the instrument? (tick)

☐ blow it   ☐ strike it   ☐ pluck it   ☐ other

❧ Write a story about the instrument you chose.

Finding your way around books

❖ Choose eight books from the bookshelf – four story books and four information books.   ❖ Find and tick.

Name of book	Title page	Author	Illustrator	Publisher	Contents	Index

❖ Look at these pages.

❖ Tick the boxes.
Colour the pictures.

The giant panda lives in China. It eats bamboo shoots.

☐ Information   ☐ Story

'Come on, Ann,' shouted Peter. 'Let's run away!'

☐ Information   ☐ Story

NO FUSS
PHOTOCOPIABLE

■SCHOLASTIC
www.scholastic.co.uk

The platypus

- Read the following information.
- Underline the named parts of the platypus.
- Use this vocabulary to label the illustration.

The platypus is a most unusual kind of mammal. Unlike other mammals which give birth to live young, the female platypus lays two soft-shelled eggs which she incubates for one to two weeks. When the eggs hatch she feeds the young with milk from her milk glands. The young do not suck upon the glands but push at them and then suck the milk which oozes out into her fur.

The platypus has a large, soft beak or bill which is so sensitive that it is able to detect the small creatures in the water which the platypus feeds upon. This sensitive beak is invaluable as the platypus is blind and deaf in the water.

The body of the platypus is furry. Its four legs have webbed feet. It uses the front legs to paddle and hind legs to swim. This enables it to swim strongly under the water. Male platypuses have a poison gland on their ankles which they use to fend off enemies. Adult platypuses weigh up to 2.4kg and males grow up to 60cm while females are slightly smaller. Platypuses are found only in parts of Australia and Tasmania.

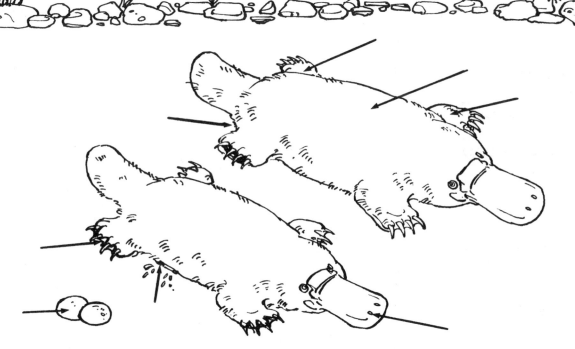

The human body

• Arrange the topic words in alphabetical order and list the related items under each topic.

eyelid　　　　breastbone

　　　scar tissue
white blood cells
　　　　　　　　　pupil
　　　EARS
　　　　　　　heartbeat
dermis
　　knee cap
　　　　　　　hip bone
　lobe
arteries
　　　　　ear canal
backbone
　　　　　eardrum
　　　iris
BLOOD　　oxygen

stirrup bone　　　　　**EYE**
epidermis

　　red blood cells　　ribcage
　deafness
　　　　　sunburn

　　　SKELETON
　　tear duct

　　　　　　freckles
　skull
　　　sweat glands
　　　　　　aorta

eyelashes
　　　SKIN
　　　　　　lens
outer ear

NO FUSS
PHOTOCOPIABLE

SCHOLASTIC
www.scholastic.co.uk

Elephants

● Read the information below and complete the chart.

Elephants are the largest living land animals. There are two different kinds of elephants – African elephants and Asian elephants. Both types of elephants have features in common and distinguishing features. Both African and Asian elephants live in herds. They have very sensitive senses of hearing and smell, but both have very poor eyesight. The African elephant has larger, rounded ears, whereas the Asian elephant's ears are smaller and more triangular in shape. The back of the African elephant has a dip or hollow, but the Asian elephant's back is rounded. Asian elephants have two bulges on their foreheads, while the African elephant's forehead is more rounded in shape. The tusks of the Asian elephant are smaller than those of the African. Finally, their nostrils, at the end of their trunks, are slightly different in shape. The African elephant has two finger-like lips which can pick up quite small objects, while the tip of the Asian elephant's trunk has only one lip.

Elephants	social grouping	senses					
African							
Asian							

Taking exercise!

Exercise is good for our bodies.
♣ Find out why and write down three reasons.

1 _____

2 _____

3 _____

Playing sport is a good way of exercising.
♣ Make a list of sports that exercise the body.

My list of sports

♣ Choose one of the sports and write about it.

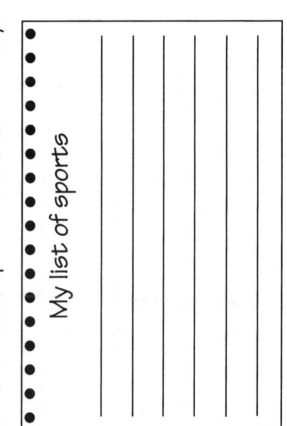

School pets

The following questions may help you.

- What are the animals' names?

- Are they male or female?

- Where do they sleep?

- What do they eat and drink?

- Who cares for them?

- Have you learned anything from them?

✿ What types of animals do you have in your school? Write about them.

✿ If you could have another pet at school, what would you choose? Why?

Making a jelly

● Read this letter and then present the information again giving clear instructions. Remember to give your writing a heading, to list the ingredients and then write out the instructions for making the jelly.

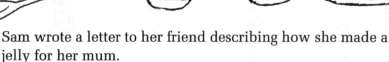

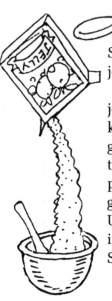

Sam wrote a letter to her friend describing how she made a jelly for her mum.

'I thought I'd give my mum a surprise, so I got a packet of jelly from the cupboard and read what I had to do. I boiled a kettle of water, but I couldn't find a measuring jug so I just guessed the pint of water. Anyway, I poured the water over the jelly and stirred it until it had melted. I thought I would put it in the fridge to set quickly. When it was supper time I got out my jelly – it had set and looked a lovely colour. Unfortunately, when my mum came to serve it, she had to cut it with a knife! She said that I had not added enough water. Still, it tasted great.'

Ingredients _____

_____

_____

_____

_____

Method _____

_____

_____

_____

_____

_____

_____

_____

_____

_____

Heraldry

● Read this passage.

When a medieval knight was in full armour his face was covered with a helmet so it was impossible to decide who he was or even for whom he was fighting! In order for his supporters to recognise him, the knight would wear a 'coat of arms'. This was a decorated tunic worn over his armour. This led to the practice of putting the same designs on the shield.

A shield was divided into nine main areas. Across the top of the shield were the 'dexter chief', the 'centre chief' and the 'sinister chief'. Below these were the 'dexter flank', the 'fess point' and the 'sinister flank'. The bottom third of the shield was divided into the 'dexter base', the 'centre base' and the 'sinister base'.
In Latin, 'dexter' means 'right' and 'sinister' means 'left', but a shield was always decorated as seen from the point of view of the knight *behind* the shield.

Only certain colours were used to paint the shield – red, blue, black, green and purple – and only two metals could be used – silver and gold. The knights also chose to divide the shield with horizontal, vertical or chevron (v-shaped) lines. Finally they added drawings of such things as dragons, eagles, dolphins, trees, flowers and weapons. When one rich family married into another their shield emblems were often combined and consequently became more complicated.

● Now decorate the shield following these instructions and using the information given above:

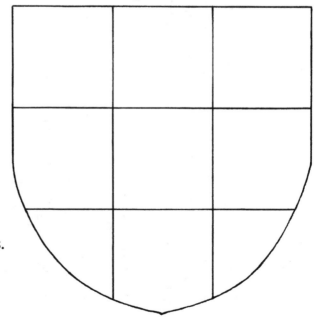

• three horizontal lines in dexter chief;
• a sun in fess point;
• three vertical lines in sinister chief;
• five horizontal lines which cover dexter base and centre base;
• two chevrons in the dexter flank;
• a rampant lion which covers sinister flank and sinister base;
• a bird in the centre chief.
(Don't forget left is right as *you* look at the shield.) Colour your shield in suitable colours.

NO FUSS
PHOTOCOPIABLE

The right order

❖ Find out what is being made on this page by placing the actions in the correct order. Read the sentences below and decide which order they should be placed in. Number each sentence then write the letter in the correct box on the right. The first one has been done for you.

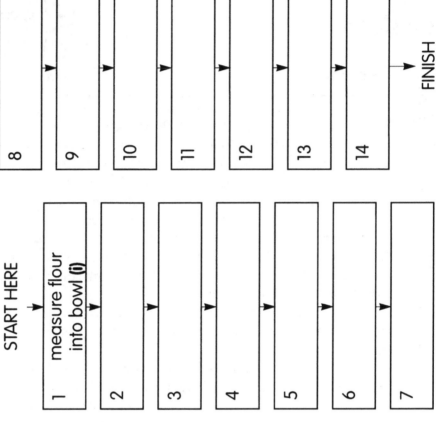

START HERE →

1 measure flour into bowl (i) →	**2** →	**3** →	**4** →	**5** →	**6** →	**7**

8 →	**9** →	**10** →	**11** →	**12** →	**13** →	**14** → FINISH

a cook second side
b whisk eggs
c put salt with flour in bowl
d eat whilst hot
e break eggs into another bowl
f heat oil in pan
g put on plate
h beat flour and eggs together into a batter
i measure flour into bowl   1.
j add milk to the eggs
k sprinkle lemon and sugar over dish
l when loose toss in pan
m shake pan
n put cupful of batter in pan

❖ Do you like to eat these on Shrove Tuesday?

❖ Why do we eat these on Shrove Tuesday?
What does 'to be shriven' mean?

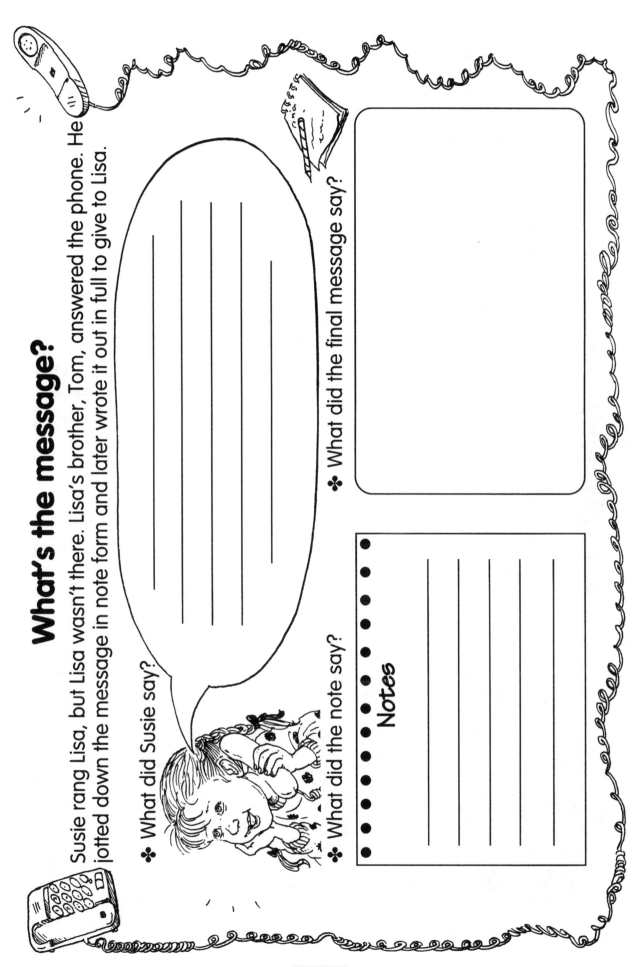

What's the message?

Susie rang Lisa, but Lisa wasn't there. Lisa's brother, Tom, answered the phone. He jotted down the message in note form and later wrote it out in full to give to Lisa.

✤ What did Susie say?

✤ What did the note say?

Notes

✤ What did the final message say?

Animal agony aunt

Wendy is an 'agony aunt' for animals. They write in with their problems and she tries to help.

✤ Answer these animal problem letters for her.

Dear Wendy,

I am the only goldfish in a big tank. I am very bored.

Can you help me?

Dear Wendy,

My owner keeps giving me treats – like double cream and fish pie. I am too fat for my basket. I can't jump over the gate or run away from dogs.

Can you help me?

A request letter

Sometimes we need to write a letter asking for a favour, or information, or because we want to buy something. Here are some words and phrases that you might choose.

♣ Select and underline the ones you want to use. Add your own ideas.

Who?	Dear Sir or Madam (if you do not know the person's name); Mr/Ms _____ (surname)
Why?	I have seen your catalogue of / advertisement in I'm writing on behalf of_____ ; on the recommendation of _____
Requesting:	Please could you send me _____ ; I would be grateful if you _____ ; We wish to ask whether _____
What?	information; prices; (further) details; free offer; answers to questions
When?	as soon as possible; by return; within _____ days; at your convenience
Enclosures:	I enclose payment; a cheque; a postal order; a stamped addressed envelope
Conclusion:	With many thanks; Yours sincerely; Yours faithfully

Signature:

Printed name:

♣ Use the words you have chosen to write your own letter.

Changing places

 parent

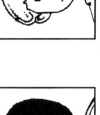 friend

 teacher

your idea

❖ Choose a person you know well.

❖ Write a diary extract as if you are that person describing your day.

Today I didn't wake up until 8 o'clock. Disaster! I knew I would be very late and I felt

Describe:

• what the person does
• where they go
• who they meet
• how they feel
• what they think about

SCHOLASTIC
www.scholastic.co.uk

The school outing

● Write a report of this school outing. You can write your report either as the headteacher or Kirsty.

8.30 a.m.   Headteacher arrives at school.

8.50 a.m.   Twenty-eight children arrive at school.

9.00 a.m.   Coach arrives at school.

9.02 a.m.   Kirsty arrives at school.

9.10 a.m.   Coach departs for castle.

9.30 a.m.   All lunches eaten by children!

9.45 a.m.   Simon requests coach stops as he feels unwell.

10.30 a.m. Coach arrives at castle.

11.30 a.m. All children have completed questionnaire

12.15 p.m. Headteacher suggests lunch – eats alone!

1.15 p.m.   Children return to coach.

1.30 p.m.   Headteacher arrives at coach.

1.45 p.m.   Peter asks coach to return, he has forgotten questionnaire.

2.30 p.m.   Coach arrives back at school.

2.45 p.m.   Parents collect children.

Fact or opinion?
'Children watch too much television.'

● Look at the statements below. Some are facts and some are
opinions. Use two coloured pencils and underline any **facts** in one
colour and any **opinions** in the other colour.

'Children definitely watch too much television these days.
A recent survey showed that quite young children are
watching over four hours of television every day. This is
obviously damaging to their health. Everyone knows that
children today take far less exercise and the television must
be to blame. There is nothing worth watching anyway and
children who watch television don't do so well at school.
It's a fact that children who watch television don't read.
They see bad behaviour on the television and this makes
them immediately go out and do the same. The
advertisements for toys and food tempt them and they're not
satisfied until they get what they want. We must stop our
children from watching this dreadful machine.'

● Make two lists headed 'Fact' and 'Opinion' and write down the
relevant text from the passage under the headings.

Fact

Opinion

_____

_____

_____

_____

_____

_____

_____

_____

SCHOLASTIC
www.scholastic.co.uk

Headline news

Newspaper headlines have to be short, simple and eye-catching.

✤ Write two different headlines for each of these crimes.

Headlines

Crime facts

Two valuable vases were stolen from the city museum by masked robbers.

A brand new car was stolen from a garage in Gear Street. Police later discovered the car, which had been burned out.

✤ List possible crime facts for these newspaper headlines.

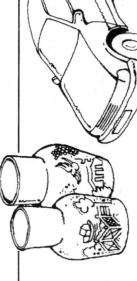

✤ Write a crime story in the form of a newspaper report. Try to include a newspaper headline, facts about the crime and a picture or photofit.

Name _____

The headline for this photograph suggests the event was great fun.

♣ Write an article about the picture.

Here are some ideas to help you:

• How many teams?
• Team names?
• What sort of boats?
• How far to race?
• What happened during the race?
• Which team won?

♣ Write a caption for the picture.

Water Weekly

The crazy boat race

◆ **Wednesday** 23 October

Newspaper headlines

- Read these news items.
- Write a headline for each article.

Firemen took three hours yesterday rescuing a small kitten that had climbed a tree. When at last Fireman Dave got hold of the kitten he received a reward – a scratch!

Once again the village held its annual flower show. As always it was a marvellous display of blooms, but the flower that held everyone's attention was the blue and white striped rose.

Peter Perkins has returned from his trip around the world in a canoe. It has taken him three years and during that time he has kept a careful diary of his adventures. Imagine his dismay when he paddled towards the harbour to see his diary blown out of the canoe and being swept away.

- Now write short articles for a newspaper under the following headlines describing what happened.

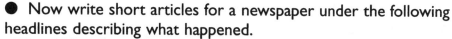 Goose saves the day!

Hurricane Henry on the way

Youngest player wins tournament

Water travel

❖ How do we travel on the water?
❖ What do we travel on?
❖ How many ways of travelling on the water can you think of?
❖ Make a list here.

❖ Choose one form of water travel and find out as much as you can about it. When was it invented? How does it move? What is it made from? What else can you find out?
❖ Write about it here.

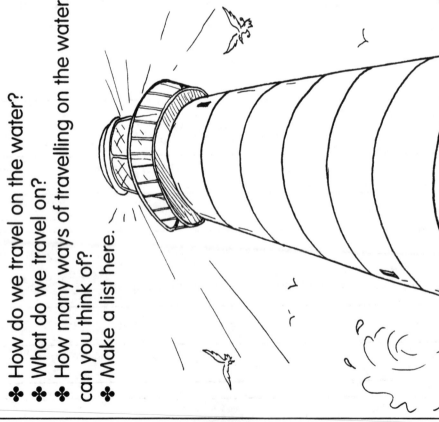

Cross-section through the Earth

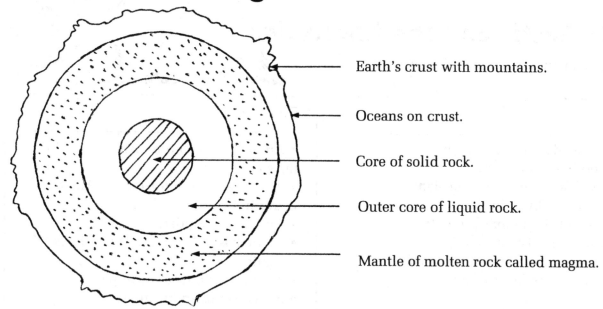

Earth's crust with mountains.

Oceans on crust.

Core of solid rock.

Outer core of liquid rock.

Mantle of molten rock called magma.

● Using the diagram above write an encyclopedia entry describing a cross-section through the Earth.

You could start your entry:

EARTH

Inside the Earth

'People once believed that the Earth was flat, but today...

_____

_____

_____

_____

_____

_____

_____

_____

_____

_____

_____

The Arctic and the Antarctic

● Look at the information below.

Same:	Different:
• long, dark freezing nights; • no light in winter; • icebergs are a common sight; • affected by pollution; • scientific stations present; • minerals discovered; • home to large number of fish; • regions are overfished.	• Arctic is in the north, Antarctic is in the south; • Arctic centre is a frozen sea, Antarctic is frozen land; • Antarctic is colder; • Arctic has polar bears, Antarctic has penguins; • Antarctic is now a world park; • minerals mined in Arctic.

● Write two paragraphs, one describing the Arctic and one describing the Antarctic, based on the information given above.

The Arctic _____

_____

_____

_____

_____

_____

The Antarctic _____

_____

_____

_____

_____

Name _____

The Hoot and Screech Club

READ THIS, IT'S IMPORTANT!

Hi! I'm Harold Hoot. Did you know that owls in Britain are having a hard time of it?

Their traditional nesting sites are disappearing _____. Woodland

is being chopped down so _____ in hollow trees becomes tricky.

Barns _____ being converted into houses or razed

_____ the ground to make way for _____

and roads. How would you feel _____ you were an owl and when

it _____ to nesting-time and you fancied _____

same home as last year, you _____ off, and when you arrived the

_____ had gone and there were no _____ suitable

homes for miles around? It _____ put you right off laying, I'm

_____.

So, how can you help? Well _____ Hoot and Screech

Club are _____ nesting boxes for suitable sites all

_____ Britain. If you know of a _____ where

an owl could nest, or want to _____ in any way get in touch with

this club. The address is on the back page of the paper.

Remember – an owl in a nest,
an owl has a rest.

Safari park poster

♣ Design an exciting poster to advertise a special day at the safari park – perhaps a 'Family Picnic Day' or a 'Safari I-Spy Tour'.

♣ Inform the public of the type of event, date, place, time, cost, attractions and so on.

♣ Make the poster clear and colourful.

The amazing snowball machine

You have invented a wonderful machine for making snowballs.

✤ Write and draw an advertisement for your machine. It should be exciting so that everyone will want to buy it.

✤ Use the back of this sheet for an advertisement for something else you have invented.

Safety rhymes

Sometimes a silly rhyme can help you to remember something important.

♣ Adapt a nursery rhyme and write a verse which reminds people about road safety.

Here is one to start you off, based on 'I hear thunder/Frère Jacques'.

I hear traffic, I hear traffic,
Rushing past, rushing past,
Wait until the road's clear,
Wait until the road's clear,
Safe at last! Safe at last!

My rhyme

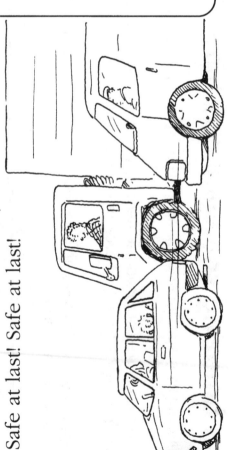

■ SCHOLASTIC
www.scholastic.co.uk

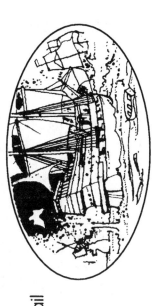

Spanish Armada report

Imagine you are an English sailor who watched the burning English galleons sail towards the Spanish Armada on 21 July 1588 at Calais.

✿ Write a description of what happened, in the form of a report, to send to Queen Elizabeth I.

Plan your ideas first. List words to describe:

how the Spanish galleons looked	what happened
how you felt	Other information
the colours, sounds and smells of the burning English galleons	

Start your report:

Your Royal Majesty, Queen Elizabeth

Police report

✤ Look carefully at this picture.

✤ Finish the police report describing what happened. Continue on the back of this sheet if you have to.

Remember that police reports just describe the facts.

Date: 4th October   Time: 4pm

I was called to the scene of an accident on

Beech Lane at 1.30pm. Mark Brown, aged 10yrs

6mths, of 2 Beech Lane had...

■ SCHOLASTIC
www.scholastic.co.uk

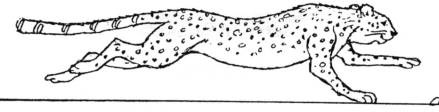

Zoos

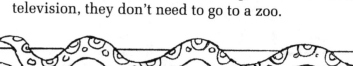

Zoos have saved many animals from extinction.
Zoos are unfair to animals.
It allows people to see animals they would never see otherwise.
The animals change in captivity, sometimes they become neurotic.
They confine animals in small spaces.
Zoos don't give the animals a natural life.
It means people can observe them and learn about them.
They have a safer life in the zoo than in the wild.
They provide entertainment for people.
They cost too much and people can't afford to go to them.
It means more people are interested in the animals.
People can see these animals living in the wild on the television, they don't need to go to a zoo.

A class of children have brainstormed about the need for zoos.
● Sort out their arguments into two columns, under the headings 'For' and 'Against'.
● Choose one side of the argument and, on the back of this sheet, write a paragraph giving your point of view.

For

Against

_____   _____
_____   _____
_____   _____
_____   _____
_____   _____
_____   _____
_____   _____
_____   _____
_____   _____
_____   _____

NO FUSS
PHOTOCOPIABLE

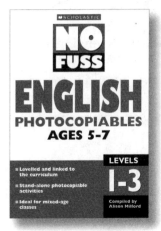

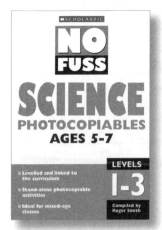
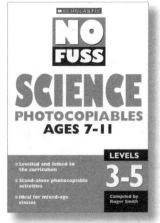